COLD CUISINE
for Entertaining

ideals

Ideals Publishing

Nashville, Tennessee

Publisher	Patricia Pingry
Cookbook Editor	Teri Mitchell
Manuscript Editor	Lise Nikora
Copy Editor	Susan DuBois
Art Director	Jennifer Rundberg
Freelance Artist	Mickey Braithwaite
Pasteup Artist	Kris Ray

ISBN 0-8249-3058-4
Copyright © MCMLXXXVI by Ideals Publishing
Previously published as *Köstliche kalte Küche*
by Ceres-Verlag, Rudolf-August Oetker KG Bielefeld, West Germany
All rights reserved.
Printed and bound in West Germany.
Published by Ideals Publishing
P.O. Box 141000
Nashville, Tennessee 37214-1000

TABLE OF CONTENTS

Appetizer Cocktails

Fruit and Shrimp Cocktail

(Illustrated previous page)
Makes 4 servings

1 banana, thinly sliced
1 apple, peeled and thinly sliced
1 to 2 tablespoons lemon juice
1 orange, peeled and sectioned
1 can pitted sour cherries, drained
12 shrimp, cooked
Lettuce leaves, washed and dried
Yogurt Dressing (recipe below)
Lemon slices
Fresh dill

Combine banana and apple slices in a large bowl. Sprinkle lemon juice over and mix well. Add orange sections. Fold in cherries and shrimp. Arrange lettuce leaves in seashells or serving dishes. Add fruit and shrimp mixture; top with Yogurt Dressing and garnish with lemon slices and dill.

Yogurt Dressing

⅔ cup plain yogurt
1 tablespoon lemon juice
Salt
White pepper
⅓ cup sliced blanched almonds, lightly toasted

In a small bowl, combine yogurt and lemon juice; mix well. Season to taste with salt and pepper. Stir in almonds.

Marinated Mushroom Cocktail

Makes 6 to 8 servings

1 pound small mushrooms, clean and dried
½ cup olive oil
2 tablespoons lemon juice
2 tablespoons vinegar
1 teaspoon salt
½ teaspoon freshly ground pepper
¼ teaspoon thyme
1 teaspoon tarragon

Combine all ingredients in a saucepan; simmer over low heat for 5 to 10 minutes. Cool; refrigerate in marinade overnight. Bring to room temperature before serving.

Exotic Fruit Cocktail

Makes 4 servings

2 medium cantaloupes
¾ cup canned lychees, drained and halved
1 ripe mango, peeled and diced
1 small jar kumquats, drained and quartered
1 to 2 tablespoons powdered sugar
3 tablespoons lemon juice
2 tablespoons orange liqueur
2 tablespoons brandy *or* kirsch
Crushed ice
Sliced kumquats *or* lychees for garnish

Cut melons in half horizontally; discard seeds. Remove most of the pulp with a melon baller; reserve shells. In a large bowl combine melon with remaining fruit. In a small bowl, combine powdered sugar with lemon juice, orange liqueur, and brandy. Pour over fruit. Cover and refrigerate for at least 1 hour. Scallop edges of reserved shells and set each on a shallow serving dish filled with crushed ice. Drain chilled fruit and spoon into shells. Garnish with kumquat slices or lychees.

Seafood Cocktail

Makes 4 servings

½ pound cooked lobster *or* crab meat, flaked
¼ cup sliced cooked mushrooms
1½ cups fresh pineapple chunks
Lettuce leaves, washed and dried
1 egg yolk
2 teaspoons prepared mustard
1 teaspoon sugar
1 to 2 tablespoons vinegar *or* lemon juice
Dash of salt
½ cup vegetable oil
4 tablespoons whipping cream
1 tablespoon sherry
Salt
Sugar
Parsley

In a medium bowl, combine lobster, mushrooms and pineapple. Arrange lettuce leaves in 4 serving dishes; top with cocktail ingredients. In a small bowl, whip the egg yolk with mustard, sugar, vinegar and salt until smooth. Continue whipping while adding oil drop by drop until mayonnaise thickens. Whip in remaining oil in a steady stream. Stir in cream and sherry. Correct seasoning with additional salt and sugar, if necessary. Spoon mayonnaise over cocktails and garnish with sprigs of parsley.

Broccoli and Cheese Cocktail

Makes 4 servings

3 cups broccoli florets
3 medium tomatoes
⅔ cup sour cream
    Pepper
    Salt
    Dill
    Lettuce leaves, washed and dried
4 to 6 ounces Camembert *or* Brie, cubed
    Chopped pistachios

In a small amount of lightly salted boiling water, cook florets for 2 to 3 minutes. Rinse under cold water and set aside to drain. Dip tomatoes in boiling water for 15 to 20 seconds; plunge into cold water, peel and remove seeds. Cut pulp into chunks. In a small bowl, combine sour cream with pepper, salt, and dill to taste. Arrange lettuce leaves in serving dishes. Divide broccoli, tomato and cheese cubes among dishes and top with sour cream. Sprinkle with pistachios.

Honeydew Cocktail

Makes 4 servings

1 honeydew melon, halved and seeded
    Sugar, optional
    Lemon juice
    Lettuce leaves, washed and dried
4 ounces smoked ham, julienned
    Zesty Dressing (recipe below)
    Mint sprigs *or* lemon balm

Remove melon pulp with a melon baller. Sprinkle with sugar and lemon juice to taste. Arrange lettuce leaves in 4 serving dishes. Add melon and ham; top with Zesty Dressing. Garnish with sprigs of mint or lemon balm.

Zesty Dressing

1 egg yolk
2 tablespoons vinegar *or* lemon juice
    Dash of salt
½ cup vegetable oil
3 tablespoons ketchup

In a small bowl, whip the egg yolk, vinegar and salt until smooth. Continue whipping while adding oil drop by drop until mayonnaise thickens. Whip in remaining oil in a steady stream. Stir in ketchup.

Broccoli and Cheese Cocktail, this page

Chicken Salad Cocktail

Makes 4 servings

8 to 10 asparagus spears, cooked
½ pound cooked chicken breast, skinned and julienned
Salt
Pepper
Lemon juice
Lettuce leaves, washed and dried
1 canned peach half, drained and chopped
Mustard Dressing (recipe below)

Cut asparagus in 1 to 1½-inch lengths. Place in a medium bowl and combine with chicken. Season to taste with salt, pepper and lemon juice. Arrange lettuce leaves in 4 serving dishes; spoon ingredients over lettuce. Prepare Mustard Dressing. Fold chopped peach into dressing and spoon over cocktails.

Mustard Dressing

1 egg yolk
1 to 2 teaspoons prepared mustard
Dash of salt
2 tablespoons vinegar *or* lemon juice
½ cup vegetable oil

In a small bowl, whip the egg yolk, mustard, salt and vinegar until smooth. Continue whipping while adding oil drop by drop until dressing thickens. Whip in remaining oil in a steady stream.

Asparagus Cocktail Hawaii

Makes 4 servings

2 large oranges
10 to 12 asparagus spears, cooked
½ pound small shrimp, cooked
6 tablespoons mayonnaise
2 tablespoons pineapple juice
Pepper
Lemon juice
Crushed ice

Cut oranges in half horizontally. Carefully remove orange sections without damaging shells. Remove membranes from sections. Reserve shells. Cut asparagus in 1½-inch lengths. In a medium bowl, combine shrimp with asparagus and orange sections. Stir pineapple juice into mayonnaise; season to taste with pepper and lemon juice. Fold into cocktail ingredients. Spoon into orange shells. Serve on crushed ice.

Mushroom-Chicken Cocktail

Makes 4 servings

½ pound mushrooms, wiped
and trimmed
Chicken broth
1 cup skinless chicken breast,
cooked and chopped
2 to 3 tablespoons lemon juice
Salt
Pepper
Lettuce leaves, washed and
dried
Creamy Dressing (recipe
below)

In a covered saucepan, cook mushrooms in a small amount of lightly salted water or boiling chicken broth until just tender (about 2 minutes); drain, cool, and slice. Combine mushrooms with chicken in a medium-sized dish; add lemon juice and seasonings to taste. Cover and refrigerate until serving time. Arrange lettuce leaves in serving dishes. Spoon chicken and mushrooms over lettuce and top with Creamy Dressing.

Creamy Dressing

1 egg yolk
1 teaspoon prepared mustard
2 teaspoons vinegar or lemon
juice
1 teaspoon sugar
½ cup vegetable oil
2 ounces cream cheese,
softened
3 tablespoons sour cream
1 teaspoon celery seed or
celery salt to taste

In a small bowl, whip the egg yolk, mustard, vinegar and sugar until smooth. Continue whipping while adding oil drop by drop until mayonnaise thickens. Whip in remaining oil in a steady stream. Set aside. In a small bowl, combine cream cheese and sour cream; blend well. Stir in mayonnaise and celery seed.

Celery Cocktail

Makes 4 servings

3 cups thinly sliced celery
6 ounces Swiss cheese, cubed
2 slices boiled ham, julienned
1⅓ cups sour cream or yogurt
Lemon juice
Worcestershire sauce
Salt
Cayenne pepper
Sliced blanched almonds,
lightly toasted
Watercress

In a medium bowl, combine celery, cheese and ham. In a small bowl, season sour cream with lemon juice, Worcestershire sauce, salt and pepper to taste and fold into cocktail ingredients. Spoon into 4 serving dishes. Sprinkle with toasted almonds and garnish with watercress.

Tuna Cocktail

Makes 4 servings

12 ounces canned tuna, drained
   and flaked
 3 shallots, finely chopped
 1 tablespoon capers
   Lettuce leaves, washed and
   dried
⅔ cup sour cream
 2 tablespoons whipping cream
 1 tablespoon prepared mustard
 1 tablespoon minced fresh dill
   or 1 teaspoon dried dill
   Worcestershire sauce
   Garlic salt
   Sugar
   Dill pickles
   Hard-boiled eggs, quartered

In a small bowl, combine tuna, shallots and capers. Arrange lettuce leaves in 4 serving dishes. Stir sour cream with cream, mustard and dill. Season to taste with Worcestershire sauce, garlic salt and sugar. Spoon cocktail over lettuce and top with dressing. May be garnished with additional capers, dill pickles and eggs.

Spring Cocktail

Makes 4 servings

12 asparagus spears, cooked
¼ pound cooked lobster or
   crab meat, flaked
   Salt
   Pepper
   Lemon juice
 3 ounces smoked ham, ju-
   lienned
16 strawberries, halved
   Lettuce leaves, washed and
   dried
 2 to 3 tablespoons mayonnaise
 2 tablespoons ketchup
 2 teaspoons lemon juice, or to
   taste
 1 to 2 tablespoons brandy, optional
   Chervil or parsley leaves

Cut asparagus into 1½-inch lengths; combine with lobster in a medium bowl. Season to taste with salt, pepper and lemon juice. Fold in ham and strawberry halves. Arrange lettuce leaves in 4 serving dishes. Top with cocktail ingredients. Mix mayonnaise with ketchup, lemon juice and brandy; spoon over cocktails. Garnish with chervil or parsley.

Tuna Cocktail, this page

Boursin and Grapes Cocktail

Makes 4 servings

¼ cup Boursin *or* other cream
   cheese
½ teaspoon evaporated skim
   milk
20 large, seedless flame red *or*
   green grapes
⅓ cup minced pistachios,
   toasted

With an electric mixer, whip cheese and
milk until smooth and fluffy. Pat about ½
teaspoon of cheese around each grape.
Place coated grapes on a flat pan in a single
layer and freeze until firm, 10 to 15 minutes. Roll grapes in pistachios. Gently cut
grapes in half with a sharp knife. Arrange
cut side up on a serving plate. Place in refrigerator until serving time.

Lobster Cocktail

Makes 4 servings

 2 tomatoes
¾ pound cooked lobster, cubed
¾ cup whole kernel corn,
   cooked and drained
 8 to 10 stuffed green olives,
   thinly sliced
⅔ cup yogurt
 1 tablespoon fresh mixed
   herbs, minced (basil, dill,
   thyme, marjoram)
   Salt
   Pepper

Dip tomatoes in boiling water for 15 to 20
seconds, plunge into cold water, peel, halve
and seed. Cut pulp into strips and combine
in a medium bowl with lobster, corn and
olives. Divide between 4 serving dishes.
Season yogurt with herbs, salt and pepper
to taste; spoon over cocktail ingredients.

Figs and Fruit Cocktail

Makes 4 servings

4 slices honeydew melon
4 slices cantaloupe *or* Casaba
   melon
12 thin slices Parma ham *or*
   Westphalian *or* prosciutto
4 fresh figs, washed and
   trimmed

Fill four shallow bowls with crushed ice.
Wrap each melon slice with a slice of ham;
distribute among bowls. Wrap each fig
with a slice of ham; center on melon slices.

Roast Beef Cocktail

Makes 4 servings

½ pound cooked roast beef
2 small dill pickles, diced
2 ounces boiled ham,
　　julienned
1 medium onion, sliced *or*
　　chopped
3 tablespoons minced chives
2 tablespoons capers
　　Salt
　　Pepper
　　Worcestershire sauce
　　Lettuce leaves, washed and
　　dried
2 hard-boiled eggs, quartered
2 slices smoked ham, halved
　　or 2 slices smoked salmon,
　　halved
½ cup sour cream
4 tablespoons mayonnaise
2 tablespoons prepared
　　mustard
2 tablespoons caviar, divided
　　or 2 tablespoons minced
　　anchovies, divided

Cut beef into bite-sized strips. Combine in a medium bowl with pickles, ham, onion, chives, and capers. Season to taste with salt, pepper, and Worcestershire sauce. Arrange lettuce leaves in 4 serving dishes. Divide cocktail ingredients among them. Garnish with eggs and ham, or smoked salmon slices twisted into spirals. In a small bowl, combine sour cream with mayonnaise and mustard. Fold in one tablespoon caviar or anchovies; spoon over the cocktails. Sprinkle with remaining caviar or anchovies.

Helpful Hints

Cluster candles of various sizes for a dramatic centerpiece. Surround with flowers, seashells or decorative accents.

Never use candles as decorations without first charring the wick.

Make ice cubes ahead of time and place in plastic bags in the freezer.

First Courses

Marinated Vegetables with Avocado Dressing

(Illustrated previous page)
Makes 4 servings

1 fennel bulb, trimmed and
   quartered
2 tablespoons lemon juice
1 large carrot, sliced
   lengthwise
2 cups broccoli florets
2 leeks, trimmed, halved
   crosswise, and rinsed
1 red bell pepper, seeded,
   halved and sliced
2 celery ribs, strings removed,
   halved crosswise
6 ounces mushrooms, trimmed
   and sliced
4 tablespoons vegetable oil
4 tablespoons white wine
   vinegar
1 onion, peeled and minced
1 garlic clove, crushed
   Salt, pepper, and sugar
   Avocado Dressing (recipe
   below)

Cook fennel in a small amount of boiling water with the lemon juice for about 7 minutes; drain and discard water. Cook carrot slices in boiling salted water for about 5 minutes; remove with a slotted spoon and set aside. In the same manner, cook broccoli for about 3 minutes, leeks for 2 to 3 minutes, pepper strips and celery for 1 to 2 minutes, and mushrooms for about 1 minute. Add more water whenever necessary. Combine all vegetables in a non-metallic bowl. Whisk together oil and vinegar, stir in onion and garlic, and season to taste with salt, pepper and sugar. Pour over vegetables and refrigerate, covered, for at least 2 hours. Spoon marinade over vegetables from time to time. To serve, arrange vegetables on a large serving platter as illustrated. Serve dressing separately.

Avocado Dressing

1 ripe avocado, peeled and
   pitted
1 tablespoon lemon juice
1 cup sour cream *or* yogurt
1 clove garlic, minced
1 tablespoon minced parsley
1 tablespoon minced chives
1 tablespoon minced dill
   Lemon juice
   Onion salt
   Salt, pepper, and sugar

In a medium bowl, mash avocado pulp with a fork; sprinkle with lemon juice. In a small bowl, combine sour cream with garlic; mix well. Add avocado and herbs; season to taste with remaining ingredients.

Lobster Toast

Makes 4 servings

3 tablespoons butter, softened
1½ tablespoons seafood cock-
    tail sauce
4 slices white sandwich bread,
    toasted
1½ tablespoons mayonnaise
1 tablespoon sour cream
2 hard-boiled eggs, peeled and
    chopped
    Salt
    White pepper
6 ounces cooked lobster,
    flaked
    Lettuce leaves, washed and
    dried
    Lemon slices
    Fresh dill or parsley

Cream butter with cocktail sauce; spread on toast. Halve toast diagonally. In a small bowl, combine mayonnaise and sour cream; add chopped eggs and season to taste with salt and pepper. Divide between toast triangles; top with flaked lobster. Arrange lettuce leaves on serving plates. Place 2 triangles on each plate and garnish with lemon slices and dill or parsley.

Avocados with Shrimp

Makes 4 servings

2 ripe avocados
2 to 3 tablespoons lemon
    juice, divided
3 tablespoons sour cream
1 tablespoon whipping cream
1 teaspoon minced dill
    Salt, pepper, and sugar
    Worcestershire sauce
3 medium tomatoes, peeled,
    seeded and diced
3 to 4 ounces cooked shrimp,
    diced
    Onion salt, optional
    Lettuce leaves, washed and
    dried
    Fresh dill or parsley

Cut avocados in half lengthwise; remove pits. Scoop out most of the pulp, leaving shells intact. Dice the pulp and sprinkle with 1 tablespoon lemon juice. In a small bowl, combine sour cream, cream and dill; season to taste with salt, pepper, sugar, lemon juice and Worcestershire sauce. Stir in tomatoes and shrimp. Sprinkle avocado shells with onion salt. Mound filling in shells. Arrange lettuce leaves on serving dishes, top with avocado halves and garnish with dill or parsley.
Variation: Fill shells with tomatoes and shrimp; top with dressing.

Escargot

Makes 4 servings

24 precooked canned snails
24 snail shells
   Canning liquid
 6 to 7 tablespoons butter, softened
½ onion, minced
 1 clove garlic, minced
 1 to 2 tablespoons minced parsley
   Salt
   Pepper

Drain snails and reserve liquid. Wash shells thoroughly in hot water; allow to drain well. Pour ½ teaspoon canning liquid in each shell; add snails. Cream butter. Add onion, garlic and parsley; season to taste with salt and pepper. Fill shells with butter mixture. Preheat oven to 400° F. Place the stuffed shells into a snail dish or into a shallow ovenproof pan filled with salt. Heat on middle rack for 10 to 12 minutes or until butter bubbles.

Note: Although a hot dish, this classic was included because it can be prepared ahead of time, refrigerated and baked at the last minute.

Bright Borscht

Makes 4 servings

 1 pound cooked beets, sliced, fresh *or* canned
 1 14½-ounce can chicken broth
¼ cup coarsely chopped red onion
 1 clove garlic
 3 to 4 tablespoons orange juice
½ cup plain yogurt *or* Neufchatel cheese, softened
 1 cucumber, diced
   Orange slices

Process or blend first 5 ingredients until smooth. Stir in yogurt and cucumber. Chill; garnish with orange slices before serving.

Escargot, this page

Eggs with Watercress Mayonnaise

Makes 4 servings

8 hard-boiled eggs, halved
½ pound cooked baby shrimp
   or prawns
   Cucumber slices
   Watercress Mayonnaise (recipe below)
   Watercress sprigs
   Lemon wedges

Divide egg halves, shrimp, and cucumber slices evenly among 4 serving dishes. Prepare Watercress Mayonnaise. Pour mayonnaise evenly over eggs and garnish with watercress and lemon wedges.

Watercress Mayonnaise

Makes 1⅓ cups dressing

1 egg
2 tablespoons white wine vinegar or lemon juice
½ cup watercress sprigs
½ cup parsley sprigs
1 green onion, sliced
2 teaspoons Dijon-style mustard
½ teaspoon tarragon leaves
½ cup safflower oil or vegetable oil
½ cup Neufchatel cheese or kefir
   Salt and freshly ground pepper to taste

Combine first 7 ingredients in a blender or food processor; blend until smooth. With machine running, add oil a few drops at a time, increasing flow to a slow, steady stream. Blend in cheese and season with salt and pepper.

Stuffed Pea Pods

Makes 4 servings

25 snow peas
¼ pound mild goat cheese (Montrachet or Lezay)
¼ cup plain yogurt
1 teaspoon prepared mustard
½ cup finely chopped spiced pecans, divided

Cut stem end of snow peas and pull down straight edge to remove any string. Blanch in boiling water for 30 seconds. Plunge peas into ice water. Using a sharp paring knife, slit open each pod along straight side. In bowl, combine cheese, yogurt, mustard, and ¼ cup pecans. Stuff each pea pod with goat cheese mixture. Dip stuffing side of each pod into remaining nuts.

Avocado Kebabs

Makes 4 servings

Tangy Mustard Dip
2 avocados, seeded, peeled,
   and cubed
Lemon juice as needed
4 ounces cheddar cheese,
   cubed
4 ounces salami, cubed
4 ounces Swiss *or* Monterey
   Jack cheese, cubed
4 cherry tomatoes *or* ripe
   olives
Red *or* green apple slices

Prepare Tangy Mustard Dip. Dip avocado cubes in lemon juice. Immediately assemble all ingredients, except Tangy Mustard Dip, on 6-inch skewers, according to ingredient list. Lay skewers across apple slices and serve with Tangy Mustard Dip.

Tangy Mustard Dip

Makes 1 cup dip

½ cup plain yogurt
½ cup cottage cheese
2 tablespoons Dijon-style
   mustard
⅛ teaspoon garlic powder

Process or blend all ingredients until smooth. Chill at least 15 minutes before serving.

Shrimp Remoulade

Makes 8 to 10 servings

4 tablespoons vegetable oil
2 tablespoons olive oil
½ teaspoon white pepper
½ teaspoon salt
1 teaspoon snipped parsley
½ teaspoon horseradish
1 celery heart, minced
2 tablespoons tarragon vinegar
4 tablespoons brown mustard
½ cup snipped green onions
1½ pounds large shrimp, cooked
   and hot

Combine all ingredients except shrimp; whip with a fork or whisk until well blended. Pour over hot shrimp. Refrigerate in marinade. Serve chilled in individual seafood shells or on a serving dish.

Herring à la Bornholm
Makes 4 servings

1 tart apple, peeled and cored
1 cup white wine
4 pickled herring fillets
4 tablespoons lingonberries, canned
⅔ cup sour cream
Fresh dill
Lingonberries

Slice apple into 4 rings and poach in pan in white wine until fork-tender but still firm enough to hold shape. Cool in liquid. Drain apple rings and arrange them on a platter. Reserve poaching liquid. Roll up herring fillets and set on apple rings edgewise. Spoon one tablespoon lingonberries into each herring roll. Stir about 2 tablespoons poaching liquid into the sour cream; spoon over berries. Garnish with dill and lingonberries.
Variation: Substitute whole cranberry sauce or currant jelly for lingonberries.

Crudités with Garlic Dip
Makes 4 servings

4 medium cloves garlic
2 large egg yolks at room temperature
⅛ teaspoon salt
¼ teaspoon Dijon-style mustard
¾ cup olive oil *or* vegetable oil
1 teaspoon lemon juice
½ teaspoon cold water
1 cup cauliflower florets, steamed
1 cup broccoli florets, steamed
4 green onions, trimmed
½ cup fresh mushrooms
4 carrots, cut into 3-inch sticks
4 stalks celery, cut into 3-inch sticks

Crush garlic and reduce it to a paste; place in a blender or food processor. Add egg yolks, salt, and mustard; blend briefly. Gradually stir in half the oil. Add lemon and water; add the remaining oil, blending slowly and steadily. Transfer to a glass serving bowl; cover and refrigerate. To serve, place dip in the center of a large platter and arrange vegetables around it.

Herring à la Bornholm, this page

24

Smoked Salmon on Green Beans

Makes 4 servings

1 pound green beans
2 tablespoons vegetable oil
2 to 3 tablespoons lemon juice
1 small onion, peeled and
  minced
½ teaspoon salt
¼ teaspoon pepper
  Sugar
4 slices smoked salmon
8 thin lemon slices
⅔ cup sour cream
  Grated rind of ½ lemon
1 tablespoon dill, minced
  Salt
  Pepper
  Fresh dill
  Lemon peel

Trim beans and cook in boiling salted water until tender-crisp (about 8 minutes). Rinse under cold running water and let cool. Place in a non-metallic bowl. Set aside. In a small bowl, whisk oil and 2 tablespoons of lemon juice. Add onion and season to taste with salt, pepper and sugar. Add more lemon juice if needed. Pour dressing over beans and marinate for about 1 hour. Arrange beans on serving plates. Drape a slice of smoked salmon over each serving. Place 2 lemon slices next to smoked salmon. In a small bowl, combine sour cream with grated lemon rind and minced dill; add salt and pepper to taste. Spoon or pipe over lemon slices. Garnish with dill and bows of lemon peel.

Mushroom-Stuffed Tomatoes

Makes 6 servings

6 medium tomatoes
  Salt
  Pepper
½ pound mushrooms, trimmed
  and sliced
1 small onion, peeled and
  minced
1½ tablespoons butter
1½ cups tiny peas, cooked and
  drained
¼ cup Green Goddess Dressing
  or mayonnaise
  Lettuce leaves, washed and
  dried
  Parsley

Slice the top off each tomato. Scoop out seeds. Sprinkle inside with salt and pepper and invert shells to drain for 10 to 15 minutes. In a small frying pan, sauté mushrooms and onion in butter for about 7 minutes. Blot with paper towels; let cool. Combine mushrooms and peas; fold in dressing. Spoon into tomato halves and arrange on a platter over lettuce. Garnish with parsley.

*Smoked Salmon on
Green Beans, this page*

26

Asparagus on Toast
Makes 4 servings

2 egg yolks
3 tablespoons lukewarm water
2 to 3 tablespoons un-
   sweetened whipped cream
Salt
Pepper
Lemon juice
12 ounces asparagus tips,
   cooked and drained
4 slices buttered toast
3 to 4 ounces smoked *or*
   boiled ham, julienned
Chopped parsley
Lettuce leaves, washed and
   dried

In a small double boiler, over simmering water, beat egg yolks and water until thick. Remove from heat and continue beating until cool. Fold in whipped cream and season with salt, pepper and lemon juice to taste. Divide asparagus between toast slices, top with dressing and sprinkle with ham and parsley. Serve on lettuce leaves.

Eggplant Caviar
Makes 8 servings

1 large eggplant, sliced in half
   lengthwise
2 tablespoons red *or* white
   wine vinegar
1 tablespoon lemon juice
1 teaspoon olive oil
¼ teaspoon ground cumin
¼ teaspoon cinnamon
⅛ teaspoon allspice
3 tablespoons minced parsley
1 clove garlic, minced
   Salt and pepper to taste
2 tomatoes, chopped
2 green onions, chopped
   Cilantro *or* parsley sprigs

Place eggplant in a shallow baking dish or on a baking sheet. Bake at 375° F for 30 minutes or until softened. In a bowl, combine vinegar, lemon juice, oil, spices, parsley, and garlic; blend well. Add salt and pepper, if desired. Dip eggplant in cold water, peel off skin, and dice pulp. Combine diced eggplant, tomatoes, and green onion. Pour dressing over vegetable mixture. Cover and chill well before serving. Garnish with cilantro.

Watermelon and Chicken Salad

Makes 4 to 6 servings

8 ounces mushrooms, trimmed
   and sliced
1 tablespoon butter
   Salt
   Pepper
   Lemon juice
4 cups watermelon balls
1¼ cups cooked chicken *or* turkey, skinned and diced
   Worcestershire *or* Tabasco
   sauce, optional
3 to 4 tablespoons mayonnaise
   Lettuce leaves, washed and
   dried
   Parsley

Sauté mushrooms in butter for about 10 minutes; season to taste with salt, pepper and lemon juice; cool. In a medium bowl, combine melon, chicken and mushrooms; season to taste with Worcestershire or a few drops of Tabasco sauce. Fold in mayonnaise. Arrange lettuce leaves on a serving platter and top with salad. Garnish with parsley.

Greek Cocktail

Makes 4 servings

1 head Boston lettuce
1 medium onion, sliced
½ medium cucumber, sliced
3 medium tomatoes
¼ cup black olives, pitted and
   sliced
8 anchovy fillets, rinsed and
   halved
4 ounces Feta cheese,
   crumbled
1 garlic clove, crushed and
   minced
½ cup sour cream *or* yogurt
   Salt
   Pepper
   Chopped chives

Wash and dry lettuce leaves and tear into bite-sized pieces; place in salad bowl. Separate onion slices into rings and add to lettuce. Add cucumber slices. Cut tomatoes into 8 wedges each. Blot with paper towels and add to salad. Mix in olives, anchovies and cheese. Stir garlic into sour cream and season to taste with salt, pepper, and chives; pour over salad ingredients. Toss and divide among 4 serving dishes.

Salami Milano

Makes 4 servings

½ pound small onions, peeled
2 tablespoons olive oil
½ teaspoon sugar
　Salt
　Pepper
½ cup white wine
2 tablespoons lemon juice
1 tablespoon tarragon vinegar
½ pound salami, sliced very
　thin
　Tomato wedges
　Mint leaves *or* lemon balm

In a small frying pan, sauté onions in oil until partially cooked. Add sugar; season to taste with salt and pepper. Cook, stirring constantly, until onions are lightly browned. Add wine, lemon juice, and vinegar; simmer for 10 to 15 minutes. Cool in liquid; drain. Arrange salami slices and onions on serving plates. Garnish with tomato wedges and mint leaves.

Ceviche

Makes 4 servings

1 pound cooked fish (mixture
　of bay shrimp, scallops, and
　squid *or* white fish fillets,
　cubed)
1 avocado, diced
2 green onions, minced
6 to 8 cherry tomatoes, halved
¼ cup lime juice
¼ cup salsa
1 teaspoon oil
1 teaspoon white *or* red wine
　vinegar
¼ teaspoon oregano leaves
1 to 2 tablespoons sliced jala-
　peno peppers *or* diced green
　chilies
1 to 2 tablespoons chopped
　cilantro
　Scallop shells, optional
　Lemon twists, optional

Marinate fish and avocado in a mixture of onion, tomatoes, lime juice, salsa, oil, vinegar, and oregano in refrigerator at least one hour or overnight. Drain and toss with peppers and cilantro. Chill before serving. Serve in scallop shells with lemon twists, if desired.

Radicchio and Asparagus Cocktail

Makes 4 servings

1 pound asparagus, cooked
   tender-crisp
1 red onion, thinly sliced
¼ pound mushrooms, wiped,
   trimmed and sliced
10 to 12 radicchio leaves,
   washed and dried
3 tablespoons olive oil
3 tablespoons lemon juice
   Salt
   Pepper
   Sprigs of dill *or* parsley

Cut asparagus into 1½-inch lengths; mix with sliced onion and mushrooms. Tear radicchio leaves into bite-sized pieces and arrange them in 4 serving dishes. Divide cocktail ingredients among the dishes. Whisk together oil and lemon juice; season with salt and pepper to taste and pour over cocktails. Garnish with dill or parsley sprigs.

Leeks Vinaigrette

Makes 5 servings

10 small leeks
1 clove garlic, peeled
3 tablespoons vegetable oil
2 tablespoons white wine
   vinegar
1 teaspoon prepared mustard
   Salt
   Pepper
2 tablespoons minced chives
1 to 2 hard-boiled eggs, peeled
   and chopped

Remove roots and wilted outer leaves of leeks; trim green tops to within 6 inches of white stalks. Partially split leeks, leaving root ends connected; wash under running water. In a medium saucepan, bring 1 quart salted water to a boil; add garlic and leeks and cook for 12 to 15 minutes. Drain, cool and arrange on serving platter. In a small bowl, whisk together oil, vinegar and mustard. Season dressing to taste with salt and pepper; stir in chives. Pour over leeks and marinate for 1 to 2 hours. Before serving, sprinkle chopped eggs over leeks.

Salads

Asparagus Mimosa

(Illustrated previous page)
Makes 4 servings

1 pound asparagus spears, cooked
6 tablespoons vegetable oil
3 tablespoons vinegar
2 small onions, minced
  Salt
  Pinch of pepper
  Sugar
3 tablespoons minced mixed herbs
  Yolk of 1 hard-boiled egg
  Chopped chives
  Watercress

Drain asparagus well, let cool and arrange on a serving platter. In a small bowl, whisk together oil and vinegar; add onion and season to taste with salt, pepper and sugar. Stir in herbs. Pour part of the dressing over asparagus; serve remainder on the side. Press egg yolk through a coarse sieve and sprinkle over asparagus; add chives. Garnish with watercress.

Mushroom Salad Deluxe

Makes about 4 servings

1 pound mushrooms, trimmed and quartered
  Salt
  Pepper
4 to 6 slices cooked roast beef, julienned
2 hard-boiled eggs, diced
4 tablespoons vegetable oil
2 tablespoons vinegar
1 to 2 tablespoons ketchup
4 tablespoons whipping cream
1 teaspoon brandy, optional
  Salt
  Pepper
  Paprika
  Sugar
2 tablespoons minced parsley

In a saucepan, cook mushrooms in a small amount of boiling water for three to five minutes; drain. Season with salt and pepper and let cool. In a serving bowl, combine mushrooms with roast beef and eggs. In a small bowl, whisk together oil, vinegar, ketchup, cream and brandy; season to taste with salt, pepper, paprika and sugar. Add minced parsley. Fold dressing into salad ingredients. Marinate, refrigerated, for 15 to 20 minutes. Correct seasoning with salt and pepper, if needed.

Vegetable Salad

Makes 5 to 6 servings

½ cup cooked peas, drained
½ cup cooked corn, drained
½ cup cooked diced carrots, drained
½ cup cooked sliced mush-rooms, drained
1 small can asparagus tips, drained and halved
1 small can sliced green beans, drained
½ red bell pepper, seeded and diced
⅓ cup mayonnaise
2 to 3 tablespoons sour cream
Salt
Pepper
1 tablespoon chopped parsley
1 tablespoon chopped chives

Combine all vegetables in a salad bowl. Mix mayonnaise and sour cream; season to taste with salt and pepper. Stir in parsley and chives. Fold into salad ingredients.

Avocado Salad

Makes 4 servings

2 avocados, peeled and pitted
Lemon juice
3 tomatoes
4 ounces mushrooms
4 slices boiled ham, julienned
2 hard-boiled eggs, diced
½ clove garlic, peeled
3 tablespoons vegetable oil
3 tablespoons whipping cream
4 tablespoons herbed vinegar
Salt
White pepper
Curry powder

Dice avocado pulp and sprinkle with lemon juice. Dip tomatoes into boiling water for about 15 seconds. Plunge into cold water, skin and quarter. Remove seeds and slice pulp. Wipe mushrooms clean; trim and slice thinly. Combine with avocados, toma-toes, ham and eggs. Wipe salad bowl with garlic. Fill with salad ingredients. In a small bowl, whisk together oil, cream and vinegar; season to taste with salt, pepper and curry powder. Fold dressing into salad and marinate for ½ hour before serving.

Bulgarian Zucchini Salad

Makes 4 to 6 servings

4 tablespoons olive oil
2 tablespoons herbed vinegar
½ teaspoon prepared mustard
    Salt, pepper, and sugar
1 tablespoon minced chives
1 tablespoon minced dill
2 medium zucchini, sliced
4 medium tomatoes, sliced
1 to 2 green bell peppers,
    seeded and cut into strips
1 medium onion, peeled and
    thinly sliced
8 to 10 pitted olives, thinly
    sliced
2 hard-boiled eggs, diced
3 to 4 ounces Feta cheese,
    crumbled

In a large salad bowl, whisk together olive oil, vinegar and mustard; season to taste with salt, pepper and sugar. Stir in chives and dill; combine with salad ingredients. Fold in eggs and half of the cheese; sprinkle remaining cheese over salad.

Chicken and Mushroom Salad

Makes about 4 servings

½ ounce dried wild mushrooms
½ cup lukewarm water
½ pound chicken breast,
    skinned and deboned
2 tablespoons vegetable oil
    Salt
    Pepper
½ pound mushrooms, trimmed
    and sliced
2 green onions, thinly sliced
    Herb Dressing (recipe below)

Soak dried mushrooms in the lukewarm water. Set aside. In a small skillet, brown chicken in oil for 2 to 3 minutes on each side or until done. Season to taste with salt and pepper. Remove from pan and let cool. Stir sliced mushrooms into pan drippings; add dried mushrooms with their soaking liquid and cook for 5 to 6 minutes. Remove from pan and let cool. Dice or julienne chicken breast; in a serving dish combine chicken with mushrooms and sliced onion. Fold in dressing and marinate for about ½ hour before serving.

Herb Dressing

1 egg yolk
1 teaspoon prepared mustard
1 tablespoon vinegar *or* lemon
   juice
1 teaspoon sugar
   Salt
   Pepper
½ cup vegetable oil
1 tablespoon sour cream
1 tablespoon cream
3 tablespoons minced basil
   leaves *or* 1 tablespoon dried
   basil

In a small bowl, whip the egg yolk, mustard, vinegar and sugar until smooth. Add salt and pepper to taste. Continue whipping while adding oil drop by drop until mayonnaise thickens. Whip in remaining oil in a steady stream. Stir sour cream, cream and basil into mayonnaise.

Mixed Salad Platter

Makes 4 to 6 servings

1 head Boston lettuce
3 to 4 medium onions, peeled
   and sliced
1 green bell pepper, halved,
   seeded and sliced
1 red bell pepper, halved,
   seeded and sliced
4 large tomatoes, cored and
   sliced
1 small cucumber, rinsed and
   sliced
1½ cups whole-kernel corn,
   cooked and drained
9½ ounces canned tuna, drained
   and flaked
⅔ cup sour cream
2 to 3 tablespoons cream
2 to 3 tablespoons ketchup
   Salt, pepper, and sugar
   Lemon juice
   Parsley, chopped
   Dill, chopped
   Chives, chopped

Discard outer lettuce leaves. Remove remaining leaves; wash and spin or pat dry. Divide larger leaves. Line a serving platter with the lettuce. Divide onion slices into rings and arrange on lettuce together with pepper strips, tomato and cucumber slices, corn and tuna. In a small bowl, mix sour cream, cream and ketchup; season to taste with salt, pepper, sugar and lemon juice. Spoon over salad. Sprinkle with chopped herbs.

Camembert Salad

Makes about 2 servings

4½ ounces Camembert, not
   too soft
4 tablespoons oil
2 tablespoons vinegar
   Salt, pepper, and sugar
1 tablespoon chopped mixed
   herbs
1 small fennel bulb, trimmed
1 tart apple, peeled, quartered
   and cored
4 to 5 leaves Boston lettuce,
   washed and dried
2 tablespoons sour cream
   Lemon juice
1 to 2 tablespoons chopped
   walnuts
   Fennel tops *or* fresh dill

Slice Camembert thickly; place in a deep serving platter. In a small bowl, whisk together oil and vinegar; season to taste with salt, pepper and sugar. Add herbs and pour dressing over cheese. Marinate for about ½ hour. Tip platter and drain dressing into a small bowl. Slice fennel thickly. Cut apple quarters into slices lengthwise. Mix with Camembert and fennel. Tear lettuce into bite-sized pieces and add to salad. Stir sour cream into dressing and correct seasoning with lemon juice if needed. Spoon over salad. Sprinkle with chopped walnuts. Garnish with fennel tops or dill.

Mussels Vinaigrette

Makes 3 to 4 servings

2 cups canned mussels, rinsed
   and drained
1 dill pickle, chopped
6 stuffed green olives, sliced
6 cocktail onions, quartered
1 cup diced tomato pulp
4 tablespoons vegetable *or*
   light olive oil
2 tablespoons red wine vinegar
1 teaspoon prepared mustard
   Salt
   Pepper
1 tablespoon minced parsley
   Lettuce leaves, washed and
   dried

In a bowl combine mussels, pickle, olives, onion, and tomato. In a small bowl, whisk together oil, vinegar and mustard; season to taste with salt and pepper. Stir in parsley. Pour dressing over salad ingredients and mix well. Arrange lettuce leaves on a serving dish; top with salad.

Camembert Salad, this page

Tuna Salad with Pineapple

Makes 4 servings

9½ ounces canned tuna, drained and flaked
1½ cups fresh pineapple, diced
¾ cup cooked peas, drained
4 tablespoons vegetable oil
2 tablespoons vinegar
1 teaspoon prepared mustard
Salt
Pepper
Sugar
1 tablespoon chopped parsley

In a serving dish, combine tuna, pineapple and peas. In a small bowl, whisk together oil, vinegar and mustard. Season to taste with salt, pepper and sugar. Add parsley. Pour over salad ingredients and mix well. *Variation:* Add 1 cup cooked, cooled rice to salad ingredients.

Turkey Salad

Makes 4 servings

¾ pound cooked turkey breast, skinned and diced
1 cup mandarin orange sections, drained
8 asparagus tips, cooked and halved
6 ounces sliced mushrooms, cooked and drained
½ cup mayonnaise
Lemon juice
Pepper

In a serving dish, combine turkey with oranges, asparagus and mushrooms. Season mayonnaise with lemon juice and pepper. Fold into salad ingredients.

Egg and Radish Salad

Makes 4 servings

⅔ cup sour cream
1 tablespoon lemon juice
Salt, pepper, and sugar
1 tablespoon chopped parsley
4 hard-boiled eggs, sliced
2 bunches radishes, washed, sliced and trimmed

In a small bowl, mix sour cream with lemon juice; season to taste with salt, pepper and sugar. Add parsley and fold in eggs and radishes.

Matjes Herring Salad

Makes 3 to 4 servings

6 matjes herring fillets
1 cup club soda *or* mineral
water
2 onions, sliced
2 to 3 dill pickles, sliced
6 ounces mushrooms, cooked
and sliced
⅔ cup sour cream
2 tablespoons whipping cream
1 to 2 teaspoons horseradish

Soak herring fillets in club soda for about 3 hours. Drain; pat dry and cut into bite-sized pieces. Separate onion slices into rings; add to herring together with pickles and mushrooms. Combine sour cream, whipping cream, and horseradish; mix well and fold into salad ingredients.

Savory Bologna Salad

Makes 4 servings

2 medium apples, peeled and
sliced
Lemon juice
½ pound Leona bologna,
skinned and sliced
2 medium dill pickles, thinly
sliced
½ cup mayonnaise
Pepper
Lettuce leaves

Sprinkle apple slices with lemon juice. In a medium bowl, combine bologna, apples and pickles; fold in mayonnaise. Correct seasoning with pepper, if needed. Serve on lettuce leaves.

Variation: Substitute your favorite salad dressing for mayonnaise.

Roast Beef Salad

Makes 4 servings

2 small onions, peeled and
thinly sliced
¾ pound cooked roast beef
8 ounces sliced canned
mushrooms, drained
3 tablespoons vegetable oil
2 tablespoons vinegar
2 to 3 tablespoons whipping
cream
Salt, pepper, and sugar

In a small pan, cook onion rings in a small amount of salted water for about 5 minutes. Drain and allow to cool. Dice or julienne meat; in a serving dish, combine with mushrooms and onion. In a small bowl, whisk together oil and vinegar; add cream and season to taste with salt, pepper and sugar. Combine with roast beef mixture.

Variation: Use venison instead of roast beef.

Cheese and Ham Salad

Makes 4 servings

8 ounces sliced Gouda, julienned
½ pound boiled ham, julienned
1 cup unsweetened pineapple tidbits, drained
½ cup mayonnaise
2 tablespoons pineapple juice
Chopped walnuts
Boston lettuce leaves, washed and dried

In a serving bowl, combine Gouda and ham; add pineapple tidbits. In a small bowl, mix mayonnaise with pineapple juice; add walnuts. Fold into salad ingredients. Serve on lettuce leaves.

Pasta and Pork Salad

Makes about 4 servings

8 ounces shell macaroni
¾ pound cooked pork roast, diced
3 tablespoons capers, drained and liquid reserved
2 to 3 tablespoons pine nuts
½ to ⅔ cup mayonnaise
½ teaspoon dried sage
Salt
Pepper
Lettuce leaves, washed and dried

In two to three quarts of boiling salted water, cook macaroni *al dente*. Rinse under cold water and drain. Let cool. In a large bowl, combine macaroni, pork, capers and pine nuts. In a small bowl, combine mayonnaise with reserved liquid from capers. Add sage and season to taste with salt and pepper. Fold into salad ingredients. Arrange lettuce leaves on serving dish. Top with pasta salad.

Waldorf Salad

Makes 4 servings

2 cups diced apples
Lemon juice
2 cups sliced celery
4 tablespoons chopped walnuts
⅓ to ½ cup mayonnaise
Boston lettuce leaves, washed and dried
Walnut halves

In a medium bowl, lightly sprinkle apples with lemon juice. Combine with celery, walnuts and mayonnaise. Arrange lettuce leaves on individual serving plates. Top with salad and garnish with walnut halves.

Mediterranean Salad

Makes about 4 servings

1 cup canned garbanzo beans, drained
1 medium onion, peeled, halved and sliced
8 to 10 tomato wedges
1 cup cooked, sliced green beans
8 slices salami, julienned
6 tablespoons olive oil
3 tablespoons red wine vinegar
1 teaspoon prepared mustard
  Salt, pepper, and sugar
1 tablespoon minced tarragon

In a salad bowl, combine vegetables and salami. In a small bowl, whisk together oil, vinegar and mustard; season to taste with salt, pepper and sugar. Stir in tarragon. Pour dressing over salad ingredients and mix. Marinate for about ½ hour before serving.

Variation: Use parsley instead of tarragon.

Parisian Salad

Makes about 4 servings

1 cup seedless green grapes, washed and halved
1 cup seedless red grapes, washed and halved
8 ounces cooked skinless chicken breast, diced
4 to 6 ounces Gouda, sliced
1 small jar mushroom slices, drained
½ cup mayonnaise
3 tablespoons yogurt
  Lemon juice
  Pepper
  Boston lettuce leaves, washed and dried
  Small bunches of grapes, washed

In a medium bowl, combine grapes, chicken, Gouda and mushrooms. In a small bowl, mix mayonnaise with yogurt; season to taste with lemon juice and pepper. Fold into salad ingredients. Serve on lettuce and garnish with small bunches of grapes.

Witches' Salad
Makes 4 servings

¾ pound ring bologna, skinned
and sliced
2 dill pickles, sliced lengthwise
2 red onions, peeled, halved
and sliced
1½ teaspoons capers
2 tomatoes
4 tablespoons vegetable *or*
walnut oil
2 tablespoons vinegar
1 to 2 teaspoons prepared
mustard
Salt
Pepper
Sugar
2 to 3 tablespoons chopped
parsley

In a salad bowl, combine bologna with pickles, onion and capers. Dip tomatoes into boiling water for about 15 seconds; plunge into cold water and skin. Cut into 8 wedges each. Add to salad ingredients. In a small bowl, whisk together oil, vinegar and mustard; season to taste with salt, pepper and sugar. Add parsley and pour dressing over salad. Marinate for ½ hour before serving.

Three Bean Salad
Makes about 4 servings

1 cup canned cut green beans,
drained
1 cup canned kidney beans,
drained
1 cup canned butter beans,
drained
½ to ⅔ cup minced red onion
4 tablespoons vegetable *or*
olive oil
2 tablespoons herbed vinegar
½ teaspoon salt
¼ teaspoon pepper
Sugar
1 tablespoon minced chives
Pinch of savory
Pinch of borage, optional

In a salad bowl, combine beans and onion. Whisk together oil and vinegar; season to taste with salt, pepper and sugar. Stir in chives, savory and borage. Pour over salad ingredients and marinate for ½ to 1 hour.

Witches' Salad, this
page

44

Corn and Shrimp Salad

Makes 4 servings

2 medium tomatoes
2 cups cooked corn, drained
8 ounces cooked shrimp
4 tablespoons vegetable oil
2 tablespoons vinegar
1 small onion, peeled and
  chopped
  Salt, pepper, and sugar
1 to 2 tablespoons minced
  chives
1 to 2 tablespoons minced
  parsley

Dip tomatoes in boiling water for about 15 seconds. Plunge into cold water and skin. Remove seeds and dice pulp. In a serving bowl, combine tomatoes with corn and shrimp. In a small bowl, whisk together oil and vinegar. Stir in onion and season to taste with salt, pepper and sugar; add chives and parsley. Fold dressing into salad. Correct seasoning if needed.

Herring Salad

Makes 4 to 6 servings

1 cup diced herring fillets
1 cup diced apples
½ cup diced cooked beets
2 cups diced boiled potatoes
½ cup diced, cooked roast
  beef, optional
2 dill pickles, diced
6 tablespoons vegetable oil
3 tablespoons red wine vinegar
1 teaspoon prepared mustard
  Salt, pepper, and sugar
1 tablespoon minced onion
1 tablespoon minced parsley
  Hard-boiled eggs
  Gherkins

In a large bowl, combine first 6 ingredients. In a small bowl, whisk together oil, vinegar and mustard; season to taste with salt, pepper and sugar. Stir in onion and parsley. Pour dressing over ingredients in bowl and mix well. Marinate for 1 hour before serving. To serve, arrange salad on a platter and garnish with wedges of hard-boiled eggs and gherkins cut into fans.

Egg Salad Excelsior

Makes 2 servings

2 hard-boiled eggs, sliced
4 slices boiled ham, julienned
½ red bell pepper, seeded and julienned
Lettuce leaves, washed and dried
⅓ cup yogurt
Salt, pepper, and sugar
Lemon juice
Worcestershire sauce
Chives, chopped

Arrange first 3 ingredients on 2 serving plates over lettuce. In a small bowl, season yogurt to taste with salt, pepper, sugar, lemon juice and Worcestershire sauce. Pour over salad ingredients. Sprinkle with chives.

Gourmet Salad

Makes about 4 servings

8 ounces cooked chicken breast, skinned
1 small can asparagus tips, drained
1 orange, peeled and white membrane removed
1 cup medium shrimp, cooked
¾ cup cooked mushroom halves, drained
1 medium dill pickle, sliced
1 tablespoon almond slivers, lightly toasted
3 tablespoons mayonnaise
2 tablespoons yogurt
1 teaspoon prepared mustard

Cut chicken, asparagus, orange and shrimp into bite-sized pieces; place in a medium salad bowl. Combine with mushroom halves, pickle and almonds. In a small bowl, mix mayonnaise with yogurt and mustard. Fold into salad ingredients.

Potato Salad

Makes about 6 servings

1½ pounds salad potatoes
½ pound cooked roast beef
1 leek, trimmed
4 ounces cooked mushrooms, quartered
3 medium tomatoes
6 tablespoons vegetable oil
4 tablespoons herbed vinegar
1 teaspoon prepared mustard
1 large onion, minced
Salt
Pepper

Cook potatoes in boiling water until done. Drain; peel and slice while still hot. Cut beef into bite-sized strips; in a large bowl, combine beef and potatoes. Cut leek in half lengthwise. Remove all but about two inches of the green tops. Wash thoroughly and slice crosswise. Add leek and mushrooms to potatoes. Dip tomatoes into boiling water for about 15 seconds; plunge into cold water and skin. Remove seeds and dice pulp; add to salad. In a small bowl, whisk together oil, vinegar and mustard. Stir in onion and season to taste with salt and pepper. Pour dressing over salad ingredients and mix carefully. Marinate salad for 1 hour before serving.

Tossed Salad

Makes about 6 servings

½ head iceberg lettuce, washed and dried
1 medium zucchini, thinly sliced
2 ribs celery, thinly sliced
2 large Kiwis, peeled and sliced
4 ounces smoked ham
4 tablespoons vegetable or walnut oil
2 tablespoons vinegar or lemon juice
Salt, pepper, and sugar
1 tablespoon minced tarragon
2 tablespoons chopped pistachios

In a salad bowl, tear lettuce leaves into bite-sized pieces; combine with zucchini and celery. Cut Kiwi slices in half. Cut ham into bite-sized strips; add Kiwi and ham to salad ingredients. In a small bowl, whisk oil and vinegar; season to taste with salt, pepper and sugar. Stir in tarragon. Toss salad with the dressing and sprinkle with pistachios.

Potato Salad, this page

Hungarian Meat Salad

Makes 4 servings

Boston *or* bibb lettuce
½ pound cooked beef, diced
1 green bell pepper, seeded
 and diced
2 hard-boiled eggs, diced
8 stuffed green olives, sliced
1 onion, peeled and sliced
8 cocktail onions, halved
4 tablespoons vegetable oil
2 tablespoons vinegar
 Salt, pepper, and sugar

Wash and dry lettuce leaves; tear into bite-sized pieces. In a salad bowl, combine lettuce, beef, pepper, eggs, olives, and onion. In a small bowl, whisk together oil and vinegar; season to taste with salt, pepper and sugar. Pour over salad and toss.

Tomato Baskets

Makes 4 to 8 servings

4 large tomatoes
1 green bell pepper, seeded
 and julienned
½ pound cooked pork roast,
 julienned
¼ pound boiled ham,
 julienned
2 tablespoons mayonnaise
2 tablespoons yogurt
1 to 2 tablespoons vinegar *or*
 lemon juice
 Salt
 Pepper
 Watercress *or* parsley

Cut tomatoes in half horizontally; scoop out seeds. Invert tomatoes to drain. In a medium saucepan, cook pepper strips in a small amount of boiling water for about 5 minutes; drain and let cool before combining with pork and ham. In a small bowl, stir mayonnaise into yogurt; add vinegar and season to taste with salt and pepper. Fold into filling ingredients and marinate for about ½ hour. Divide filling between tomato halves. Arrange tomatoes on a platter and decorate with watercress or parsley.

Grilled Goat Cheese and Walnut Salad with Mango Dressing

Makes 4 servings

1 head radicchio
1 head butter lettuce
1 head Arugula
4 to 6 ounces mild herbed goat cheese
½ cup walnut *or* hazelnut oil *or* vegetable oil
1 tablespoon mango chutney
1 tablespoon plain yogurt
2 teaspoons red wine vinegar
1 cup coarsely chopped walnuts

Discard any outer leaves, then wash and pat dry all greens. Refrigerate. Slice cheese into four chunks. Grill or broil briefly and set aside. Process or blend next 4 ingredients for dressing. To compose salad, arrange lettuce leaves on a platter. Form a ring of Arugula over lettuce. Place cheese, pinwheel fashion, in center. Sprinkle with walnuts and drizzle on dressing.

Pasta and Ham Salad

Makes 4 to 6 servings

1 cup peeled diced apples
Lemon juice
2 cups elbow *or* shell macaroni, cooked *al dente*
⅔ cup chopped dill pickles
½ pound boiled ham, diced
½ cup sour cream
2 tablespoons whipping cream
1 tablespoon ketchup
1 tablespoon minced chives
1 tablespoon minced parsley
Salt
Pepper

In a salad bowl, sprinkle apples with lemon juice; combine with macaroni, pickles and ham. In a small bowl, blend sour cream with cream and ketchup; add chives and parsley and season to taste with salt and pepper. Fold into salad ingredients.

Crab Louis Salad

Makes 4 servings

½ cup Minceur Mayonnaise
  (recipe below)
½ cup plain yogurt
¼ cup half-and-half
¼ cup chili sauce
 1 teaspoon Worcestershire
  sauce
 1 clove garlic, minced
  Dash hot pepper sauce
 2 tablespoons lemon juice
¼ cup minced green pepper
¼ cup minced onion
 2 cups shredded iceberg lettuce
 1 to 2 cups cooked flaked crab
  meat *or* small cooked shrimp

In a bowl, combine all ingredients except the lettuce and crab meat. Blend well. Arrange lettuce in a small bowl. Arrange crab meat over lettuce. Drizzle dressing over crab meat and lettuce.

Minceur Mayonnaise

Makes 1 cup dressing

 2 egg yolks
 1 tablespoon Dijon-style
  mustard
 2 teaspoons white wine vinegar *or* lemon juice
½ cup safflower oil
½ cup Neufchatel cheese *or*
  Kefir
  Salt and freshly ground pepper to taste

Combine egg yolks and mustard in a blender or food processor. With motor running, slowly add vinegar drop by drop. Drizzle in oil, slowly increasing flow to a slow, steady stream. Blend in cheese. Season with salt and pepper.

Boston Lettuce Salad

Makes 4 servings

½ cup sour cream
¼ cup Italian salad dressing
 2 tablespoons mayonnaise *or*
  salad dressing
 1 teaspoon snipped parsley
 2 small heads Boston lettuce
¼ cup shredded cheddar cheese

Combine sour cream, salad dressing, mayonnaise and parsley in a mixing bowl. Core lettuce; cut each head in half. Arrange lettuce on salad plates; top with dressing. Sprinkle with cheese.

Rice and Shrimp Salad

Makes 4 servings

2 cups cooked long-grain rice
½ pound small shrimp, cooked
½ cup diced Swiss cheese
½ cup diced tomato pulp
1 to 2 tablespoons minced onion
4 tablespoons vegetable *or* walnut oil
2 tablespoons white wine vinegar
Salt
Pepper

In a salad bowl, combine first 5 ingredients. In a small bowl, whisk together oil and vinegar; season to taste with salt and pepper. Pour dressing over salad ingredients and toss. Add a little more vinegar if needed.

Summer Salad Board

Makes 4 servings

Lettuce leaves
Watercress Mayonnaise Dip (recipe below)
2 cups sliced fresh peaches
2 cups sliced fresh pears
1 fresh pineapple, cut into 1-inch chunks
1 pint fresh strawberries
10 to 12 frozen cooked shrimp, thawed
2 cups broccoli florets

Line a large serving platter with lettuce leaves. Place a bowl of Watercress Mayonnaise Dip in the center of the tray. Arrange fruit, shrimp, and broccoli on lettuce. Provide wooden picks or forks for dipping.

Watercress Mayonnaise Dip

Makes 1 cup dip

1 bunch watercress, minced
3 tablespoons lemon juice
¼ teaspoon tarragon leaves
1 clove garlic, minced
1 cup Minceur Mayonnaise (see page 52)

In a small bowl, combine all ingredients; blend well.

Turkey Pasta Salad

Makes 6 servings

2 cups pasta wheels *or* shells
⅛ teaspoon cayenne pepper
¾ teaspoon salt
2 cloves garlic, crushed
¾ cup French dressing
2½ cups cooked turkey, julienned
½ cup diced green *or* red bell pepper
2 tablespoons sliced green olives
2 tablespoons sliced black olives
Lettuce leaves
3 hard-boiled eggs, cut into wedges
2 tomatoes, cut into wedges

Boil pasta in salted water until just tender; drain well. Mix cayenne pepper, salt, garlic and French dressing; toss hot pasta generously with half of mixture. Gently mix in turkey, pepper and olives. Add more dressing to taste. Line serving platter or individual plates with lettuce leaves. Garnish with eggs and tomatoes. Pass remaining dressing at table. Refrigerate until serving time.

Fisherman's Salad

Makes 4 servings

¾ pound shrimp, cooked
4 hard-boiled eggs
1 cup chopped parsley *or* chives
1 1-pound can tiny beets, drained
Lemon juice
2 to 3 tablespoons chopped dill
1⅓ cups sour cream
Salt
Pepper

Mound shrimp in center of serving platter. Chop whites of eggs and press yolks through a coarse sieve; alternately arrange around shrimp. Place a wreath of parsley or chives around eggs. Circle with beets. Sprinkle beets with a little lemon juice. Stir dill into sour cream; season to taste with salt and pepper. Serve separately.
Variation: Replace chopped parsley with washed peppergrass or watercress.

Shrimp and Macaroni Salad

Makes 4 servings

3 cups cooked macaroni
¼ green bell pepper, minced
3 stalks celery, diced
¼ cup finely chopped onion
2 tablespoons lemon juice
¼ cup plain yogurt
¼ cup mayonnaise
2 tablespoons minced dill
   pickle
1 tablespoon prepared mustard
1 teaspoon sugar
1 teaspoon salt
6 ounces cooked shrimp
4 hard-boiled eggs, diced

In a medium bowl, combine macaroni, green pepper, celery, onion, and lemon juice. In a small bowl, blend yogurt, mayonnaise, pickle, mustard, sugar, and salt. Blend into vegetable-macaroni mixture; add shrimp and eggs. Chill before serving.

Celeriac Tarts

Makes 4 to 8 servings

8 slices cooked celeriac
   Lemon juice
   Salt
2 hard-boiled eggs, diced
1 large pickle, diced
3 ounces boiled ham, diced
   Cooked celeriac trimmings,
   diced
½ cup mayonnaise
   Lettuce leaves, washed and
   dried
   Vinaigrette Dressing
   Parsley

Trim celeriac slices to even size with a cookie cutter or glass. Sprinkle with lemon juice and season to taste with salt. Reserve trimmings. In a small bowl, combine eggs, pickle, ham and trimmings with mayonnaise; mound on celeriac slices. Arrange lettuce leaves on serving dish and sprinkle with Vinaigrette Dressing; add celeriac tarts and garnish with parsley.

Patés, Terrines, and Aspics

Patés and Terrines

A paté is well-seasoned forcemeat encased in a crust. The crust can be puff pastry or yeast dough, depending on the type of filling.

Patés are baked in standard paté molds or on baking sheets. They can be served warm as a main course, or cold as an appetizer or as part of a cold buffet.

Terrines, on the other hand, are just the filling. They are baked in covered ovenproof dishes set in a water bath. Terrines are delicious as appetizers and should always be part of a cold buffet.

Terrines have to be weighted while cooling. This is easily done by placing a double layer of foil on top of the uncovered terrine, followed by a piece of heavy cardboard on the foil. Lay 2 bricks on top of terrine until cooled.

Paté en Croute

(Illustrated previous page)
Makes about 8 servings

Crust
2 pounds venison, trimmed and cubed
3 tablespoons walnut oil
3 tablespoons butter
2 onions, peeled and minced
8 ounces fresh bacon, cubed
4 eggs
¼ cup Madeira
⅓ cup coarsely chopped pistachios
1 teaspoon thyme
2 teaspoons salt, *or* to taste
¼ teaspoon pepper
1 pork tenderloin, rubbed with salt and pepper
1 to 2 tablespoons vegetable oil
Thin slices of fresh pork fat back *or* parboiled salt pork
1 egg, separated

Prepare crust at least 2 hours before assembling paté. Rinse meat; pat dry. In a large skillet, heat oil and butter; sauté onion until limp. Add meat in 2 batches and brown; remove from heat. Grind with bacon as finely as possible, preferably in a food processor. Mix thoroughly with 4 eggs, Madeira, pistachios and seasonings. In a skillet, brown tenderloin in hot oil on all sides. Let cool. Preheat oven to 375° F. On a lightly floured surface, roll out ⅔ of the crust dough to fit a straight-sided 11 x 4-inch sandwich loaf pan. Allow edges to hang over about 1 inch. Add half the ground meat. Wrap tenderloin in slices of fat and place in center of filling. Add remaining ground meat in an even layer. Fold overhanging dough over paté and brush with lightly beaten egg white. Roll out remaining dough to form a lid. Place on top of paté and firmly press down along edges. Cut scraps into decorative shapes; brush underside with egg white; arrange on lid. Cut a steam hole in center of lid. Brush dough with lightly beaten egg yolk. Bake for about 1¼ hours, or until fat bubbling in steam hole is clear. Cool to room temperature and refrigerate in pan.

Crust

3½ cups flour
1 teaspoon salt
1 egg yolk
7 to 8 tablespoons ice water
4 ounces butter, chilled
4 ounces lard, chilled

Sift flour and salt into a large bowl; make a well in center. Lightly beat egg yolk with 7 tablespoons of water. Pour into well and combine with some of the flour to form a thin paste. Top paste with butter and lard cut into small pieces. Cover with remaining flour and work from the center with a fork until dough starts to hold together. Add a little more water if needed. Transfer to a lightly floured work surface and knead as quickly as possible into a smooth dough. Wrap in plastic or foil and refrigerate for about 2 hours.

Liver Terrine
Makes about 10 servings

2 pounds pork liver, trimmed
  and cubed
1 pound fresh pork fat *or*
  parboiled salt pork, cubed
1 onion, peeled and minced
6 ounces cooked mushrooms,
  diced
1 tablespoon chopped parsley
1 teaspoon dried marjoram
½ teaspoon nutmeg
2 teaspoons salt
  Pepper
  Thin slices of fresh pork fat
  or parboiled salt pork
  Wine Aspic glaze, optional

Grind liver and fat in food processor. Thoroughly mix with onion, mushrooms, parsley, marjoram and nutmeg; season to taste with salt and pepper. Line a straight-sided, 1½-quart rectangular ovenproof mold with overlapping slices of fat. Allow a 1-inch overhang. Add filling. Tap form on work surface to set filling. Fold over the overhang and cover filling with more sliced fat. Cover form. If form does not have a cover, use heavy-duty foil; seal tightly. Preheat oven to 350° F. Set terrine in a larger pan containing boiling water. Water should cover ½ to ⅔ of the sides of the terrine. Bake for about 1¼ hours or until fat runs clear. Remove from oven; uncover. Place a piece of foil on baked terrine and weight down. Allow to cool at room temperature. Chill, still weighted, for at least 24 hours before unmolding. May be glazed with Wine Aspic (see page 68).

Mediterranean-Style Aspic

Makes about 6 servings

2 envelopes unflavored gelatin
⅓ cup cold water
3 cups well-seasoned beef
   stock
¼ cup white wine
¼ cup white wine vinegar
   Worcestershire sauce
10 ounces Feta cheese, preferably Bulgarian
2 ounces butter, softened
3 tablespoons whipping cream
1 tablespoon chopped green
   bell pepper
   Dried basil
6 thin slices boiled ham
1 cup small peas, cooked and
   drained
1 cup corn, cooked and
   drained
   Parsley
   Lemon slices

Sprinkle gelatin over cold water; set in a larger container with hot water until dissolved. Heat part of the stock to almost boiling; stir in gelatin. Combine with remaining stock, wine and vinegar, and season to taste with Worcestershire sauce. Mash cheese with a fork; cream with butter and whipping cream. Stir in green pepper and basil to taste. With wet hands, on a board rinsed with cold water, shape cheese into a roll to fit a six-cup loaf pan. Chill briefly. Rinse loaf pan with cold water. Cover bottom with about ⅓ inch of aspic; refrigerate until set. Arrange ham slices in an overlapping row the length of the cheese roll. Place roll on top and wrap in ham. Place in center of aspic, seam side down. Arrange peas and corn around roll and pour in remaining aspic; refrigerate. Shortly before serving, dip pan briefly in hot water, loosen edges with a knife and invert mold onto serving platter. Decorate with parsley and lemon slices.

Smoked Salmon Paté

Makes 10 servings

2 3-ounce packages smoked
   salmon, chopped
2 8-ounce packages Neufchatel
   cheese
2 to 3 cloves garlic, minced
2 to 3 green onions, minced
1 to 2 tablespoons dry vermouth
   Caviar, watercress, minced
   green onion, and minced
   parsley

Blend salmon and cream cheese in a blender or food processor until smooth. Add garlic, green onion, and vermouth; blend well. Mound in a serving bowl; chill. Garnish with caviar, watercress, minced green onion, and parsley. Serve with vegetables or crackers.

Pork Terrine
Makes about 10 servings

1 pound pork tenderloin,
  trimmed and cubed
1 pound fresh pork fat *or*
  parboiled salt pork, cubed
2 teaspoons salt
¼ teaspoon pepper
2 eggs
1 onion, peeled and minced
¼ teaspoon dried thyme
¼ teaspoon dried sage
2 tablespoons chopped parsley
¼ cup Madeira *or* brandy
1 cup sliced mushrooms
⅓ cup chopped pistachios
  Thin slices of fresh pork fat
  or parboiled salt pork
5 ounces ham, cubed *or* cut in
  strips
1 bay leaf

Grind tenderloin and fat as finely as possible, preferably with a food processor; season to taste with salt and pepper. In a bowl, mix tenderloin thoroughly with eggs, onion, herbs, wine, mushrooms and nuts. Preheat oven to 350° F. Line a 1½-quart terrine or loaf pan with overlapping slices of fat. Spoon in half of the forcemeat. Arrange ham on top and add remaining forcemeat. Press firmly. Fold fat overhang over terrine; place bay leaf on top. Cover pan tightly with foil and seal. Place in a larger pan containing boiling water. Bake for 1½ to 2 hours or until fat runs clear. Remove cover and bay leaf; drain fat. Weight terrine and let cool at room temperature. Chill for at least 24 hours before unmolding.

Stock for Aspic
Makes about 1 quart

1 pound beef *or* veal bones,
  chopped
½ pound beef shank *or* 1
  pound chicken bones,
  chopped
1 pound chicken parts (wings,
  necks, backs) *or* 1 pound
  fish bones
½ pound fish
6 cups salted water
1 rib celery
  Parsley
1 parsnip
1 small bay leaf
3 to 4 peppercorns

Rinse bones and meat well; place in a stockpot with the water. Bring to a boil and remove scum. Add remaining ingredients, return to boil and simmer, partially covered, for 2 to 2½ hours for beef stock, about 1½ hours for chicken stock and 1 to 1½ hours for fish stock. Strain through a fine sieve lined with washed cheesecloth. Let cool at room temperature, uncovered. Cover and chill in refrigerator until fat is congealed. Remove all fat before using for aspic.

Fish in Aspic

Makes 4 to 6 servings

2 cups water
½ teaspoon salt
1 rib celery
1 small onion, peeled
Parsley
1 bay leaf
2 to 3 peppercorns
1 pound fish fillets
3 tablespoons vinegar
Salt
1 envelope unflavored gelatin
3 tablespoons cold water
Cucumber slices, halved *or*
quartered
Tomato slices, halved *or*
quartered
Olive slices
Parsley
Lemon wedges

Combine first 7 ingredients in a large saucepan; bring to a boil and simmer for about 15 minutes. Add fish, return to boiling and simmer for 10 to 15 minutes more or until fish flakes easily. Remove fish from liquid and set aside to cool. Strain liquid through washed cheesecloth. Cool and degrease completely. Add cold water to make 1½ cups liquid; stir in vinegar and season to taste with salt. Sprinkle gelatin over cold water. Set in a larger container with hot water until dissolved. Bring part of the stock to almost boiling, stir in gelatin and combine with remaining stock. Rinse a 3½-cup mold with cold water. Cover bottom with aspic and refrigerate until set. Arrange cucumber, tomato and olive slices, and parsley over aspic. Add a thin layer of aspic and refrigerate until set. Arrange fish in mold and add remaining aspic. Keep refrigerated. Shortly before serving, dip mold briefly in hot water. Loosen edges with a knife and invert mold onto serving plate. Garnish with parsley and lemon wedges.

Tomato Aspic Salad

Makes 4 servings

1 envelope lemon-flavored gelatin dissolved in ½ cup boiling water
1½ cups tomato juice
1 tablespoon red·wine vinegar
Lettuce leaves

In a medium bowl, combine all ingredients except lettuce. Spray 4 small bowls with release agent; divide mixture between bowls and refrigerate until set. Unmold onto lettuce leaves.

Fish in Aspic, this page

Chicken Breast in Sherry Aspic

Makes 4 to 5 servings

2 envelopes unflavored gelatin
⅓ cup cold water
3 cups well-seasoned chicken stock
½ cup dry sherry
3 tablespoons lemon juice
Salt
Pepper
3 skinned and boneless chicken breast halves, cooked
⅓ cup cooked carrot slices
⅓ cup cooked mushroom slices
Parsley leaves
½ cup finely chopped celery
Watercress
Orange sections

Sprinkle gelatin over cold water. Set in a larger container with hot water until dissolved. Heat part of the stock not quite to boiling; stir in gelatin. Combine with remaining stock, sherry and lemon juice. Correct seasoning with salt and pepper. Trim chicken breasts. Be careful to remove all fat. Rinse a 1½-quart mold or bowl with cold water. Pour in a thin layer of aspic; refrigerate until set. Arrange a few carrot slices, mushrooms and parsley leaves over set aspic in a pretty pattern. Add a thin layer of aspic; refrigerate. Slice chicken breasts crosswise and arrange overlapping slices in a sunburst fashion over aspic. Garnish with carrot slices and chopped celery. Add another layer of aspic; refrigerate. Sprinkle remaining vegetables over mold and fill with remaining aspic. Keep refrigerated. Shortly before serving, dip mold briefly in hot water. Run a knife along the edges and invert onto serving plate. Garnish with watercress and orange sections.

Herb Cheese Mold

Makes 6 servings

1 8-ounce package Neufchatel cheese, softened
2 to 3 tablespoons lemon juice
½ teaspoon freshly ground pepper
2 tablespoons minced parsley
1 clove garlic, minced
¼ teaspoon each of 4 herbs of your choice
Skim milk

In a small mixing bowl, combine cheese, lemon juice, pepper, parsley, and garlic. Add herbs, tasting mixture with each addition. Beat cheese mixture until smooth, adding milk to thin, if necessary. Mound in a small serving bowl, press into a greased mold, or shape as desired. Cover and chill well before serving.

Crab and Avocado Aspic

Makes 5 to 6 servings

1 tablespoon unflavored
gelatin
¾ cup cold water, divided
1 cup canned consommé
1 cup cocktail vegetable juice
1 avocado, peeled and pitted
Lemon juice
1 6½-ounce can white crabmeat, drained
Watercress
Wedges of hard-boiled egg

Sprinkle gelatin over ¼ cup water. Set in a larger container with hot water until dissolved. Bring remaining ½ cup water to a boil. Remove from heat and stir in gelatin. Add to consommé and vegetable juice. Rinse a 3½-cup mold with cold water. Pour in a thin layer of aspic; refrigerate until set. Cut avocado into thin wedges. Halve wedges; reserve a few pieces and arrange rest on mold in sunburst fashion. Cover with thin layer of aspic; return to refrigerator to set. In a small bowl, dice remaining avocado, sprinkle with lemon juice; flake crabmeat and mix with diced avocado. Add a layer to mold, cover with aspic and refrigerate until set. Repeat until all crabmeat and aspic has been used. Keep refrigerated. Shortly before serving, dip mold into hot water for a few seconds, loosen edges with a knife and invert mold onto serving plate. Garnish with watercress and egg wedges.

Vegetable Fromage

Makes 4 servings

2 8-ounce packages cream
cheese
¼ cup plain yogurt
¼ cup shredded carrot
¼ cup finely chopped radish
¼ cup finely chopped red bell
pepper
¼ cup finely chopped green
bell pepper
¼ cup finely sliced green onion
or cilantro
Whole-grain breadsticks

Process all ingredients, or blend well with a wooden spoon. Use immediately or refrigerate, covered, up to 2 days. Bring to room temperature before serving with whole-grain breadsticks.

Chicken Liver Terrine

Makes about 2 cups

1 tablespoon butter
2 to 3 tablespoons chopped
  onion
1 pound chicken livers,
  trimmed
⅓ cup well-seasoned chicken
  broth
1 cup unsalted butter, cubed
1 tablespoon sherry
¼ cup whipping cream
2 slices very crisp bacon
½ teaspoon pepper
1 teaspoon salt
¼ teaspoon basil
  Pinch of coriander
  Grated rind of 1 large lemon
  Wine Aspic (see page 68)

In a medium skillet, heat butter and sauté onion until transparent. Add chicken livers and broth; simmer, covered, for 10 to 12 minutes. Turn livers once or twice during cooking; drain. In food processor, combine livers with remaining ingredients. Process with metal blade until smooth. Transfer to a bowl and chill for 15 to 20 minutes. Cream well; correct seasoning with salt and pepper. Pour mixture into a serving dish; cover with plastic or foil and refrigerate. Terrine may be covered with aspic. Refrigerate at least 4 hours before serving.

Ham in Herbed Aspic

Makes 5 to 6 servings

3¼ cups beef stock
1 onion, peeled and halved
1 clove garlic, peeled
1 clove
1 bay leaf
3 sprigs parsley, chopped
  Pinch of sage
  Pinch of thyme
  Pinch of coriander
2 envelopes unflavored gelatin
⅓ cup cold water
2 tablespoons brandy
⅓ cup port
  Salt
  Pepper
1½ to 2 pounds ham steak, fully
  cooked, trimmed and cubed
½ to ⅔ cup chopped parsley

In a large saucepan, combine stock with next 8 ingredients. Bring to a boil and simmer, covered, for about 15 minutes; strain. Sprinkle gelatin over cold water; set in a larger container with hot water until dissolved. Stir into hot stock; add brandy and port. Correct seasoning with salt and pepper; cool. Rinse a 1½- to 2-quart mold with cold water. Spoon in a layer of aspic; refrigerate until set. Alternately add layers of ham, chopped parsley and aspic. Refrigerate after each addition of aspic. Keep refrigerated. Shortly before serving, dip mold into hot water for a few seconds. Run a knife around the edges and invert mold onto serving platter. Serve with rye bread and butter.

Eggs in Aspic
Makes 6 servings

2 envelopes unflavored gelatin
⅓ cup cold water
3½ cups well-seasoned stock, divided
2 to 3 sprigs tarragon, optional
1 carrot, peeled and sliced
2 to 3 stuffed olives, sliced
Parsley
3 hard-boiled eggs, peeled and thickly sliced
Pickle slices, quartered
1 to 2 slices of boiled ham, chopped
Washed lettuce leaves *or* watercress
Tomato wedges

Sprinkle gelatin over water and place in a larger container with hot water until completely dissolved. In a small saucepan, heat 1 cup of the stock with the tarragon and carrot slices. Simmer for about 7 minutes or until carrot is tender-crisp. Strain and discard tarragon. Stir gelatin into strained stock; add to remaining stock. Rinse 6 custard cups with cold water. Spoon aspic into each cup to cover bottom. Refrigerate until set. Arrange carrot slices, olives and parsley over firm aspic. Cover with a thin layer of aspic and return to refrigerator. Repeat this process with egg slices, pickles and ham. End with a layer of aspic. Refrigerate until set. Shortly before serving, dip the cups briefly into hot water, loosen edges carefully with a knife and invert molds onto serving plates. Garnish with lettuce and tomato wedges.

Clams in Aspic
Makes 5 to 6 servings

2 envelopes unflavored gelatin
⅓ cup cold water
3 cups clam juice
¼ cup fresh lemon juice
⅓ cup white wine
2 10-ounce cans small clams, drained
⅔ cup tiny peas, cooked and drained
Parsley
Lemon slices

Sprinkle gelatin over cold water. Set in a larger container with hot water until completely dissolved. Heat part of the clam juice not quite to boiling. Stir in gelatin and combine with remaining clam juice, lemon juice and wine. Rinse a 1½-quart mold with cold water. Cover bottom of mold with a thin layer of aspic; refrigerate until set. Combine clams and peas. Add to mold alternately with layers of aspic. Refrigerate after each addition of aspic. Keep chilled. Shortly before serving, dip mold briefly in hot water. Loosen edges with a knife and invert mold onto a serving plate. Garnish with parsley and lemon slices.

Cottage Cheese and Vegetable Terrine
Makes 8 to 10 servings

2 broccoli stalks with florets
1 leek
   Instant chicken bouillon
½ pound green beans, trimmed
6 slender carrots, scraped
4 slices bacon
2 onions, peeled and chopped
4 slices sandwich bread, crusts
   removed and cubed
2 pounds dry cottage cheese
¾ cup half-and-half
4 eggs
   Salt
   Pepper
   Vegetable oil
   Watercress or parsley

Trim broccoli. Separate florets from stalks; chop stalks. Trim leek roots. Cut off green parts to within 3 inches of stalks. Cut in half lengthwise and rinse well. In a saucepan using a small amount of boiling bouillon, cook beans for 8 to 10 minutes, carrots for about 8 minutes, leek for 3 minutes, and broccoli for 3 minutes. Drain vegetables well; keep separated. Cut bacon into very fine strips. Fry in a skillet on moderate heat until bacon becomes opaque. Add onion and cook until limp. Add cubed bread and toast lightly. Remove from heat. Cream cottage cheese with half-and-half. Stir in eggs and the bacon mixture; season well with salt and pepper. Preheat oven to 400° F. Brush a 1½-quart loaf pan with vegetable oil. Separate layers of leek and line pan with the layers. Add ¼ of the cottage cheese; top with broccoli. Repeat this process with carrots and beans. End with cottage cheese. Tap pan firmly on work surface to set filling. Cover pan tightly with foil. Cut a steam hole in center. Set pan in a larger one containing hot water. Bake for 1½ to 1¾ hours. Weight terrine and cool completely before unmolding. Garnish with watercress or parsley.

Wine Aspic
Makes 2 cups

1 envelope unflavored gelatin
3 tablespoons cold water
1½ cups stock
¼ to ½ cup Madeira, sherry or
   white wine

Sprinkle gelatin over cold water. Place in a larger container with hot water until dissolved. Heat part of the stock to almost boiling, stir in gelatin and combine with remaining stock. Add wine. Can be used for glazing terrines, meats, poultry or fish.

Cottage Cheese and
Vegetable Terrine, this
page

Ham Rolls in Aspic

Makes 5 servings

2 envelopes unflavored gelatin
3¾ cups well-seasoned beef stock, divided
2 tablespoons white wine vinegar
Worcestershire sauce
8 ounces ring bologna, peeled and finely chopped
Mayonnaise *or* sandwich spread
Capers
5 slices boiled ham
2 hard-boiled eggs, sliced
Parsley leaves
1 large dill pickle, cut into thin spears
Lettuce leaves, washed and dried
Tomato wedges
Parsley

Sprinkle gelatin over ⅓ cup stock. Set in a larger container with hot water until dissolved. Heat ⅔ cup of the remaining stock to almost boiling; stir in gelatin. Combine with balance of stock and vinegar; season to taste with Worcestershire sauce. Rinse five 4½-inch ovenproof bowls with cold water. Cover bottoms of bowls with a thin layer of aspic and refrigerate until set. Combine bologna with enough mayonnaise or sandwich spread to bind; add capers to taste. Divide bologna mixture among the ham slices; roll up slices and trim ends. Arrange egg slices and parsley leaves on set aspic; top with ham rolls. Place pickle spears beside ham rolls. Add enough aspic to cover; return to refrigerator until set. When set, add any remaining aspic and keep refrigerated. Shortly before serving, dip bowls briefly in hot water. Loosen edges with a knife and invert bowls onto individual serving plates lined with lettuce leaves. Garnish with tomato wedges and parsley sprigs.

Mousse of Pike

Makes 8 servings

4 sprigs parsley, minced
1 medium onion, minced
½ teaspoon crumbled tarragon
1 envelope unflavored gelatin
½ cup warm water
2 pounds pike fillets, cooked, cooled, and puréed
1 cup heavy cream, whipped
1 cup mayonnaise

Add parsley, onion, and tarragon to a large mixing bowl. Dissolve gelatin in warm water. Let stand for 5 minutes. Add fish purée to parsley mixture 2 cups at a time until well mixed. Fold in cream and mayonnaise. Pour into an oiled 9 x 5-inch loaf pan. Cover with aluminum foil. Chill until set, about 4 to 6 hours. Unmold onto a serving platter. Slice and serve.

Smoked Trout in Aspic

Makes 6 servings

1 envelope unflavored gelatin
1½ cups well-seasoned beef
   stock, divided
¼ cup white wine
1 tablespoon white wine
   vinegar
   Salt
   Pepper
   Tabasco sauce
6 medium smoked trout fillets
2 hard-boiled eggs, sliced
2 tomatoes, sliced
6 asparagus tips, cooked
   Fresh dill *or* parsley
   Horseradish Cream (see
   page 166)

In a small bowl, sprinkle gelatin over ¼ cup of the stock. Place in a larger container with hot water until dissolved. In a saucepan, bring about half of the remaining stock almost to a boil; stir in gelatin. Combine with remaining stock, wine and vinegar. Correct seasoning with salt, pepper and a few drops of Tabasco. Refrigerate until cooled. In six soup plates, arrange trout, egg and tomato slices, asparagus tips and dill or parsley. Cover with aspic. Refrigerate until set. Serve with Horseradish Cream.

Jellied Loaf

Makes 4 to 6 servings

4 cups chicken stock
3 cups shredded cooked
   chicken
½ cup sugar
½ cup cider vinegar
½ cup thinly sliced celery
1 green pepper, thinly sliced
½ cup sliced green salad olives
¼ teaspoon pepper
1 teaspoon seasoned salt
1 teaspoon Worcestershire
   sauce
4 tablespoons unflavored gelatin, softened in ¼ cup cold
   water
   Lettuce leaves
   Mayonnaise

Place all ingredients except lettuce and mayonnaise in boiling chicken stock. Simmer for 25 minutes. Pour in a large greased or oiled loaf pan or 2 small pans. Place in refrigerator. When well-chilled and firm, unmold and slice. Place lettuce leaves on platter, top with loaf slices, and garnish with mayonnaise.

Shrimp Paté

Makes 8 servings

Butter
1 medium onion, minced
4 tablespoons butter
2½ pounds small shrimp,
    shelled and deveined
1 tablespoon dry sherry
4 sprigs parsley, minced
3 cups heavy cream
1 teaspoon salt
½ teaspoon white pepper
½ teaspoon ground nutmeg

Butter a 9 x 5 x 3-inch loaf pan. Preheat oven to 300° F. Sauté onion in butter for 2 minutes. Add shrimp; sauté until shrimp are done. Remove shrimp from heat; cool. Sprinkle sherry over shrimp; mince. Add parsley along with remaining ingredients to shrimp; blend thoroughly. Pack mixture into prepared pan. Cover with oiled aluminum foil. Place pan in a larger pan; fill outer pan with 2 inches of water. Bake 1 hour and 10 minutes or until paté is set. Cool to room temperature. Refrigerate until ready to serve. Unmold onto a serving platter. Slice and serve.

Paté with Pistachios

Makes 8 servings

¾ pound veal, minced
¾ pound pork, minced
½ pound chicken livers,
    minced
½ pound pork fat, minced
3 tablespoons butter
3 cloves garlic, minced
1 medium onion, minced
2 eggs, lightly beaten
¼ cup brandy or white wine
1½ cups pistachio nuts, shelled
    and skins removed
½ teaspoon each of thyme, all-
    spice, cinnamon, salt, and
    pepper
½ pound sliced bacon,
    blanched

Combine first 4 ingredients in large mixing bowl. Heat butter in a large frying pan. Add garlic and onion; sauté for 2 minutes. Stir in meat mixture. Stir in eggs, wine, nuts, and spices. Remove from heat. Preheat oven to 350° F. Drape bacon slices over the bottom and up the sides of a 4-cup terrine. Spoon meat mixture into the terrine; smooth top. Fold bacon strips over the top. Cover terrine with aluminum foil. Place terrine in a pan that is 2 inches larger. Pour in 2 inches of hot water. Bake for 1½ hours, until juices run clear; drain. Cool to room temperature. Chill overnight. Serve from the terrine or unmold onto a serving plate. Serve with thin slices of bread and cocktail-size pickles. Paté can be stored for 1 week tightly wrapped.

Chicken Liver Paté

Makes about 6 cups

½ cup rendered chicken fat
1 tablespoon unflavored
   gelatin
½ cup butter *or* margarine
1 cup chopped onion
1 cup chopped celery
1 cup chopped mushrooms
1½ pounds chicken livers
2 teaspoons salt
½ teaspoon pepper
¼ teaspoon garlic powder
½ cup sherry

In a heavy saucepan, combine fat, gelatin, butter, onion, celery, mushrooms, and chicken livers. Cook over low heat until tender, about 30 minutes. Add salt, pepper, garlic, and sherry. Purée in blender or food grinder. Chill in refrigerator for 3 to 4 hours.

Tangy Sausage and Veal Paté

Makes 8 servings

½ pound bacon, blanched
4 sprigs parsley, minced
½ cup bread crumbs
½ cup milk
1 medium onion, minced
3 cloves garlic, minced
1¼ pounds veal, minced
¾ pound pork, minced
1¼ pounds mildly spiced
   sausage with casing removed, minced
2 eggs, lightly beaten
⅓ cup cognac
½ teaspoon crushed thyme
4 large bay leaves

Line a 9 x 5-inch loaf pan with bacon strips; reserve 2 strips bacon for topping. Place parsley and bread crumbs in a mixing bowl. Add milk to bread crumbs; mix well. Add onion and garlic to bread crumbs; stir to combine. Add veal, pork and sausage to mixing bowl. Add eggs, cognac, and thyme to mixing bowl; mix well. Pack paté into prepared loaf pan. Arrange bay leaves on top. Cover with remaining bacon strips. Cover with aluminum foil. Place loaf pan in a larger pan. Fill outside pan with 2 inches of hot water. Preheat oven to 325° F. Bake paté for 2 hours, until juices are clear; drain. Cool to room temperature. Chill overnight. Remove bay leaves. Unmold onto a serving platter. Slice thinly and serve with crisp French bread.

Sandwiches, Nibbles, and Cheeses

Radish Sandwich

(Illustrated previous page)
Makes about 3 servings

1⅓ cups small curd cottage
    cheese
2 to 3 tablespoons whipping
    cream
1 tablespoon lemon juice
2 tablespoons minced chives,
    divided
    Salt
    Pepper
1 bunch radishes, washed and
    trimmed
    Butter
    Whole-wheat *or* rye bread,
    sliced

Combine cottage cheese, cream and lemon juice in a blender jar and blend on high until smooth. Remove jar and add one tablespoon chives. Season to taste with salt and pepper. Reserve a few radishes for garnish; slice half of the remaining radishes and set aside. Chop the other half and fold into cottage cheese. Butter bread, cover with cottage cheese and top with radish slices. Sprinkle with remaining chives. Garnish with radish roses.

Stuffed Peppers

Makes 4 to 6 servings

1 medium red bell pepper
1 medium green bell pepper
1 medium yellow bell pepper
3 hard-boiled eggs
7 tablespoons butter at room
    temperature
6 ounces cream cheese at
    room temperature
⅔ cup sour cream
    Prepared mustard
    Salt
    Pepper
    Paprika
    Pumpernickel bread

Cut off the stem ends of peppers; scrape out seeds and white membrane. Chop egg whites very finely; rice egg yolks. In a small bowl, cream butter and cheese; stir in sour cream and eggs. Season to taste with mustard, salt, pepper and paprika. Fill peppers with cheese mixture; wrap in plastic or foil and refrigerate for at least 8 hours. Shortly before serving, cut peppers into ½-inch slices. Serve with pumpernickel.

Savory Beef Rolls

Makes 4 to 8 servings

8 slices cooked roast beef
8 slices boiled ham
⅛ pound Braunschweiger
1 tablespoon whipping cream
   or 1 tablespoon brandy
½ cup vegetable oil
5 tablespoons red wine vinegar
1 teaspoon salt
1 clove garlic, crushed
1 tablespoon dried thyme
   Lettuce leaves, washed and
   dried

Trim beef and ham to even size. Cream Braunschweiger with cream or brandy and spread thinly over beef slices. Top with ham and roll up. Divide each roll into two and secure with toothpicks; place rolls in a bowl. In a small bowl, whisk together oil, vinegar and salt. Add garlic and thyme and pour over beef rolls. Marinate, covered, for at least 8 hours. Keep refrigerated. Shortly before serving, remove beef rolls and drain. Arrange on a platter over lettuce leaves. Goes well with a tossed salad and French bread.

Ribbon Wedges

Makes 24 wedges

6 tablespoons mayonnaise
14 ounces cream cheese,
   softened
   Salt
   Pepper
2 to 3 tablespoons minced
   mixed herbs
1 to 2 tablespoons tomato
   paste
   Paprika
1 teaspoon prepared mustard
   or to taste
12 thin slices of dark bread,
   crusts removed

In a small bowl, cream mayonnaise and cream cheese; season to taste with salt and pepper. Divide into three bowls. Add herbs to one bowl, tomato paste with paprika to taste to another, and mustard to the third. Spread one slice of bread with herb cheese mixture, one with tomato mixture, and the third with mustard mixture. Assemble and top with a plain slice of bread. Lightly press together. Repeat with remaining bread and cheese. Wrap sandwiches in plastic or foil and refrigerate for several hours. To serve, quarter sandwiches and halve quarters diagonally.

Filled Brie

Makes about 8 servings

1 8-ounce round Brie
4 ounces soft cream cheese
2 teaspoons currant jelly
Salt
Pepper
⅓ cup whipping cream, stiffly
  beaten
⅓ to ½ cup broken walnut
  pieces
Walnut halves

Cut Brie in half horizontally. In a small bowl, mix cream cheese and currant jelly until smooth; season to taste with salt and pepper. Fold whipped cream into cheese mixture; season to taste. Spread half of the cream cheese over the bottom half of Brie; top with broken walnuts. Replace top half of Brie and press lightly. Spread or pipe remaining cream cheese over Brie and decorate with walnut halves. Serve in wedges.

Cheese and Kiwi Canapés

Makes about ½ cup spread

4 ounces cream cheese,
  softened
2 tablespoons sour cream
Grated lemon rind
Pepper
Round crackers
1 Kiwi

In a small bowl, stir cream cheese and sour cream until smooth; season to taste with lemon rind and pepper. Generously spread or pipe on crackers. Peel Kiwi and halve horizontally. Slice each half crosswise. Press slices upright into cheese, cut side down.

Smoked Salmon and Kiwi Sandwiches

Makes 4 servings

Butter
4 slices dark sandwich bread
4 Boston lettuce leaves,
  washed and dried
8 slices smoked salmon
1 to 2 Kiwis, peeled and sliced

Butter bread and top with one lettuce leaf each. Arrange smoked salmon and Kiwi slices over lettuce.
Variation: Use your favorite creamy salad dressing or mayonnaise instead of butter.

Fisherman's Toast

Makes 2 servings

Butter
2 slices toast
1 to 2 cans sardines in oil,
  drained
  Lemon juice
  Pepper
2 hard-boiled eggs, peeled and
  sliced
  Onion rings *or* anchovy
  fillets
  Parsley

Butter toast. Arrange sardines over toast and sprinkle with lemon juice and pepper. Top with overlapping egg slices; garnish with onions or anchovy fillets and parsley.

Apple Rings with Paté

Makes about 8 slices

2 small tart apples, peeled
  and cored
  Juice of 1 lemon
2 to 3 tablespoons cold water
5 ounces liver paté
  Olives stuffed with almonds
  or chopped pistachios

Cut apples into rings not quite ½ inch thick. Dip in lemon juice mixed with water; dry on paper towels. Thickly cover with paté. Scallop edges with a cookie cutter the size of apple rings. Garnish with olives or pistachios.

Roast Beef Sandwiches

Makes 4 servings

4 onions, peeled and sliced
4 tablespoons vegetable oil
  Butter
4 slices rye bread
8 slices cooked roast beef
4 tablespoons horseradish
  Tomato wedges
  Parsley

Sauté onions in the oil until golden; drain on paper towels. Butter bread and cover with two slices of beef each. Spread horseradish over beef and arrange onion slices on top. Serve with tomato wedges and parsley for garnish.

Orange and Cheese Rounds

Makes 8 rounds

1 to 2 large oranges
8 slices whole-wheat bread
  Butter
8 slices Roquefort
  Orange peel, cut in spirals

Remove orange peel and white membrane; slice oranges thinly. Cut bread into rounds the size of the orange slices; spread with butter. Top each round with one orange slice and a piece of Roquefort. Garnish with orange peel spirals.

Smoked Trout Squares

Makes 4 to 8 servings

  Butter
2 slices dark sandwich bread
3 to 4 smoked trout fillets, small to medium size
  Lemon triangles
  Fresh dill

Butter bread and cut into quarters. Top each quarter with a piece of trout fillet and garnish with small lemon triangles and dill.

Roast Beef Rounds

Makes 8 rounds

  Mustard butter
8 2½-inch rye bread rounds
4 slices cooked roast beef, halved
  Capers

Spread mustard butter on bread. Top with roast beef slices folded to fit bread. Place capers into folds.
Variation: Substitute pastrami or corned beef for roast beef.

Cottage Cheese with Caraway Seed

Makes 4 servings

2 cups cottage cheese
4 tablespoons sour cream
1 generous teaspoon caraway seed *or* to taste
  Salt
  Pepper
  Lettuce cups

Mix cottage cheese with sour cream and caraway seed; season to taste with salt and pepper. Serve in lettuce cups.

Orange and Cheese Rounds, this page; Smoked Trout Squares, this page; Roast Beef Rounds, this page

Smoked Salmon Canapés

Makes 10 canapés

2 tablespoons unsalted butter, softened
½ tablespoon lemon juice
Grated lemon rind
Salt
Pepper
10 2-inch rounds of sandwich bread, toasted
5 slices smoked salmon, halved
Horseradish
Boston lettuce leaves, washed and dried
Lemon slices, halved *or* quartered
Fresh dill

In a small bowl, cream butter and lemon juice; season to taste with lemon rind, salt and pepper. Spread on bread rounds. Add smoked salmon, folded to fit canapés. Top with a small dab of horseradish. Arrange on a platter over lettuce leaves. Garnish with lemon and dill.

Canapés with Chicken Breast

Makes 10 canapés

1 boneless chicken breast, skinned and halved
Salt
Pepper
1 tablespoon cooking oil
1 tablespoon margarine
2 to 3 tablespoons mayonnaise
Horseradish
10 2-inch rounds of sandwich bread, toasted
Sliced toasted almonds

Season chicken to taste with salt and pepper. Heat oil and margarine in a small skillet and brown meat for about 3 minutes on each side or until done. Drain on a paper towel; let cool and slice thinly crosswise. Season mayonnaise with horseradish to taste. Use parchment paper to form a small cone; leave only a small opening at tip. Spoon mayonnaise into cone and pipe small amounts over toast rounds. Add one slice of chicken, a little more mayonnaise and top with another chicken slice. Pipe rest of mayonnaise over top for garnish and sprinkle with almonds.

Veal Scallops on Toast with Hollandaise Sauce

Makes 4 servings

4 slices sandwich bread
Butter
3 to 4 tablespoons margarine
2 tablespoons cooking oil
12 small veal scallops
Salt
Pepper
Parsley, chopped
Hollandaise Sauce (recipe below)

Cut bread into rounds. Heat butter in a skillet and toast bread on both sides. Set aside. In another skillet, heat margarine and oil. Cook scallops for about 1 minute on each side. Do not overcook. Season to taste with salt and pepper. Remove from pan to cool. Arrange 3 scallops on each round of toast; sprinkle with parsley and top with Hollandaise Sauce.

Hollandaise Sauce

3 egg yolks
1 teaspoon tarragon vinegar
1 tablespoon lemon juice
¼ teaspoon salt
Pinch of pepper
Pinch of sugar
½ pound melted butter

In a blender jar, combine egg yolks, vinegar, lemon juice, salt, pepper and sugar; blend on low until smooth. With motor still running, add melted butter in a steady stream. If not used immediately, place Hollandaise in a jar and keep warm in a saucepan with a small amount of hot water. Do not reheat sauce.

Prosciutto Canapés

Makes 10 canapés

Butter *or* mustard butter
10 2-inch rounds of sandwich bread, toasted
5 slices prosciutto, halved
Yolks of 2 hard-boiled eggs, riced
Mint *or* parsley

Butter toast rounds. Fold ham slices to fit canapés; top with egg yolk. Garnish with mint leaves or parsley.

Balkan-Style Cottage Cheese

Makes about 4 servings

1 cup cottage cheese
½ cup sour cream
1 garlic clove, minced
1 green onion, minced
½ cup peeled and finely diced cucumber
½ cup peeled, seeded and finely diced tomato
Salt
Pepper
Coriander
Parsley

In a small bowl, mix cottage cheese and sour cream. Stir in garlic, onion, cucumber and tomato; season to taste with salt, pepper and coriander. Chill and garnish with parsley.

Turkey Sandwich

Makes 1 serving

1 slice white bread, lightly toasted
Curry Dressing (see page 162)
3 slices turkey breast
Avocado slices
Lemon juice

Spread toast generously with Curry Dressing. Cut turkey breast to size of bread; place on top of dressing. Cut in half diagonally. Sprinkle avocado with lemon juice; arrange on turkey triangles.

Cheddar and Chive Balls

Makes about 15 balls

4 ounces cream cheese at room temperature
½ cup sharp cold-pack cheddar cheese
Worcestershire sauce or Tabasco sauce
½ cup finely chopped chives

In a small bowl, mash cream cheese with a fork; combine with cheddar. Season to taste with Worcestershire sauce or a few drops of Tabasco. With moist hands form 1½-inch balls; roll in chives. Refrigerate.

Garnished Ham Sandwich

Makes 4 servings

4 tablespoons butter, softened
1 tablespoon prepared mustard
2 teaspoons horseradish
4 slices rye bread
8 slices boiled *or* baked ham
4 dill pickles, cut into fans
  Cocktail onions
  Marinated baby corn
  Marinated peppers, hot *or* mild
  Radish roses
  Parsley

In a small bowl, cream butter, mustard and horseradish; spread on bread slices. Arrange two slices of ham on each sandwich; top with a pickle fan. Serve with garnishes.

Swedish Tidbits

Makes 8 tidbits

  Butter
2 slices whole-wheat bread
2 tablespoons chopped chives
1 12-ounce jar marinated herring tidbits, drained
1 onion, peeled and sliced
  Green peppercorns, crushed

Butter bread and sprinkle with chives. Cut into quarters. Arrange herring tidbits on bread, top with onion rings and sprinkle with green peppercorns.

Herbed Cottage Cheese

Makes 2 servings

8 ounces cottage cheese
4 tablespoons sour cream
  Salt
2 tablespoons minced chives *or* 2 tablespoons minced mixed herbs
  Lettuce leaves, washed and dried

In a small bowl, blend cottage cheese and sour cream; season to taste with salt. Stir in chives or herbs. Serve on lettuce leaves.

Feta Cheese in Oil

Makes 4 to 6 servings

10 ounces Feta cheese, cubed
1 to 2 red onions, peeled and
   sliced
1 to 2 yellow onions, peeled
   and sliced
1 clove garlic, peeled
1 cup pitted black olives,
   drained
2 bay leaves
3 chili peppers
1 teaspoon dried oregano
   Salt
   Pepper
1 cup olive oil

In a bowl or jar, combine first 8 ingredients; add salt and pepper to taste. Add oil to bowl and marinate, covered, for about 7 days. Keep refrigerated.

Ham and Melon Canapés

Makes 10 canapés

   Butter
10 2-inch rounds of sandwich
   bread, toasted
 5 thin slices of ham, halved
10 honeydew melon balls
   Pepper, optional

Butter toast rounds. Top with ham folded to fit canapés. Place one melon ball in center; secure with toothpick. Sprinkle with pepper.

Roquefort Balls

Makes 8 to 10 balls

4 ounces Roquefort, crumbled
4 tablespoons butter at room
   temperature, creamed
1 teaspoon minced capers
1 teaspoon brandy, optional
   Pepper
   Pumpernickel crumbs or
   chopped walnuts
   Parsley

Mash cheese with a fork and blend with butter; add capers and brandy. Season to taste with pepper. Form small balls; roll in pumpernickel crumbs or chopped walnuts. Refrigerate. Serve garnished with parsley.

Feta Cheese in Oil, this
page

Herbed Canapé Spread

Makes about ⅔ cup spread

4 ounces cream cheese,
    softened
4 tablespoons sour cream
    Salt
    Pepper
    Paprika
1 teaspoon minced parsley
1 teaspoon minced chives

In a small bowl, mix cream cheese and sour cream until smooth; season to taste with salt, pepper and paprika. Stir in minced herbs. Spread or pipe on canapé bases or crackers and garnish.

Garnishes: capers, cucumber slices, hard-boiled egg slices, sliced stuffed olives, chopped hot or mild peppers, radish slices, parsley, or peppergrass

Creamy Camembert

Makes about 1½ cups spread

½ pound ripe Camembert,
    crust removed
6 ounces unsalted butter at
    room temperature
1 to 2 shallots, peeled and
    minced
½ to 1 teaspoon Dijon-style
    mustard
    Paprika
    Toast points *or* crackers

Allow cheese to soften at room temperature, mash with a fork and mix well with the butter. Stir in onions and mustard and season to taste with paprika. Serve with toast points or crackers.

Tomato Cottage Cheese

Makes 2 servings

1 cup cottage cheese
2 tablespoons sour cream
2 tablespoons tomato paste
    Salt
    Pepper
1 green onion, minced *or* 2
    tablespoons minced mixed
    herbs

Blend cottage cheese, sour cream and tomato paste. Season to taste with salt and pepper. Stir in minced onion or herbs.

Fried Camembert
Makes about 12 cubes

½ pound package chilled Camembert, not too ripe
1 egg, lightly beaten
Finely crushed bread crumbs
Vegetable oil

Cube Camembert. Dip in beaten egg. Coat on all sides with bread crumbs; press crumbs into cheese. Repeat dipping and coating. In a small, heavy saucepan, heat oil to about 375° F. With a fork or skewer, dip cubes into hot oil, one at a time, until golden. Do not allow cheese to ooze out. Drain and place on serving plate. Serve hot or at room temperature.

Garnished Open BLT Sandwich
Makes 4 servings

Butter
4 slices toast
Garlic powder
8 Boston lettuce leaves, washed and dried
4 small tomatoes, thinly sliced
Salt
8 slices crisp bacon
2 canned *or* fresh pineapple rings, halved
4 large stuffed olives

Butter toast and lightly sprinkle with garlic powder. Arrange two lettuce leaves on each piece of toast, add tomato slices and sprinkle with salt to taste. Place two bacon slices on top. Spear halved pineapple rings and olives on four toothpicks; stand upright in center of sandwiches.

Salami Cones
Makes 12 cones

12 thin slices hard salami
Horseradish Cream (see page 166)
Parsley

Remove skin from salami. Roll slices into cone shapes; secure with toothpicks. Pipe or spoon horseradish cream into cones. Garnish with parsley leaves.
Variation: Thin slices of mortadella, ham or turkey breast, cut into rounds or oblongs, can be used instead of salami.

Asparagus Toast

Makes 4 servings

Butter
4 slices toast
4 slices cooked roast beef *or* ham
20 green *or* white asparagus tips
4 tablespoons mayonnaise
2 tablespoons whipping cream
Lemon juice
4 orange *or* mandarin orange sections
Parsley

Butter toast and top with roast beef or ham. Arrange asparagus on top. In a small bowl, blend mayonnaise and cream; correct seasoning with lemon juice. Spoon over asparagus; garnish with orange sections and parsley.

Deli Squares

Makes 4 to 8 servings

Butter
2 slices dark bread, crusts removed
8 thin cucumber slices
Salt
Pepper
Dill, chopped
1 to 2 tablespoons mayonnaise
8 medium shrimp, cooked and peeled
Fresh dill

Butter and quarter bread. Place one cucumber slice on each square, sprinkle with salt, pepper and dill to taste. Add a dab of mayonnaise topped with one shrimp. Garnish with fresh dill.

Canapé Spread

Makes about ½ cup spread

4 ounces cream cheese, softened
3 tablespoons sour cream
Yolk of 1 hard-boiled egg, riced
Lemon juice
Celery salt
Pepper
Tabasco sauce

In a small bowl, mash cream cheese with a fork; blend in sour cream. Add egg yolk and season to taste with lemon juice, celery salt, pepper and a few drops of Tabasco. Spread or pipe on crackers or canapé bases. Garnish.
Garnishes: carrot daisies, caviar, sweet gherkins, chopped peppers, olive slices, parsley, relish, or truffle strips

Asparagus Toast, this page

Dilled Shrimp on Avocados
Makes 4 servings

3 tablespoons cream cheese, softened
3 tablespoons mayonnaise
1 teaspoon lemon juice
1/8 to 1/4 teaspoon dried dill
1 tablespoon minced parsley
2 tablespoons minced green onion
1 pound small bay shrimp, cooked
2 avocados, halved
4 butter lettuce leaves
4 sprigs green onion
4 cherry tomatoes

Cream first 4 ingredients. Fold in parsley, onion, and shrimp. Cover and refrigerate at least 30 minutes. Top each avocado half with an equal portion of shrimp mixture. Serve on lettuce leaf. Garnish with green onion and tomato.

Dilled Cucumber Rounds
Makes 8 servings

1 cucumber
4 ounces Neufchatel cheese *or* kefir
1 tablespoon butter
Skim milk, heated
Salt and freshly ground pepper to taste
1/4 cup chopped pimiento-stuffed olives
2 tablespoons minced parsley *or* green onions
1/2 teaspoon minced dill
Melba toast

Cut ends off cucumbers and core inside with a sharp knife or vegetable peeler. Stand on paper towels about 1 hour to drain. Pound the cheese and butter together, adding milk to thin, if necessary. Season with salt and pepper. Stir in olives, parsley, and dill. Using a pastry bag or small spoon, fill center of cucumber with cheese mixture. Wrap in plastic wrap and chill at least 30 minutes. Slice into thick rounds. Serve on Melba toast.

Cornucopia Ham Rolls

Makes 4 servings

1 3-ounce package cream
    cheese
2 to 3 tablespoons finely
    chopped ginger
    preserves
½ cup finely chopped pecans
2 to 3 tablespoons milk
    Freshly ground black pepper
12 ham slices

Combine cheese, preserves, and pecans. Stir in milk to moisten, and season to taste. Spread over ham slices and roll up into cornucopias.

Shrimp Sandwich

Makes 1 serving

⅔ cup (3 ounces) canned
    shrimp, drained
2 tablespoons mayonnaise
    Dash garlic powder
2 slices bread
4 slices cucumber
1 large mushroom, sliced
1 slice tomato
    Alfalfa sprouts
    Seasoning salt

In a small bowl, mix shrimp with mayonnaise; season with garlic powder. Toast bread. Place cucumber slices on the bottom piece of bread. Spread shrimp mixture on top of the sliced cucumbers. Top with mushroom slices, tomato slice, and sprouts. Sprinkle with seasoning salt. Top with remaining bread.

Caviar and Olive Toast Rounds

Makes 4 servings

¼ cup caviar
10 to 12 stuffed green olives,
    finely chopped
1 to 2 tablespoons minced red
    onion
2 to 3 tablespoons lemon juice
    Melba toast rounds
3 hard-boiled egg yolks, sieved

Mix first 4 ingredients. Spread on toast rounds and sprinkle with sieved yolks.

Fish and Shellfish

Classic Crawfish Dinner

(Illustrated previous page)
Makes 5 to 6 servings

Although this dish is served warm, it has been included in this book because it is prepared ahead of time and needs a minimum of preparation time just before serving.

5 quarts water
6 tablespoons salt
2 to 3 tablespoons dill seed
½ teaspoon caraway seed
2 medium onions, peeled and
　quartered
1 celery rib
6 sprigs parsley
¼ teaspoon thyme
¼ teaspoon basil
4 pounds live crawfish
　Fresh dill
　French bread

In a stockpot, bring water, salt and seeds to a boil. Add onion, celery and herbs; boil for about 5 minutes. Add crawfish 2 at a time, head first. Return water to boiling after each addition. Simmer for about 10 minutes. Remove crawfish to a large bowl lined with dill. Strain hot liquid over crawfish; chill for about 12 hours. Shortly before serving, reheat crawfish briefly in their liquid. Remove to a warm platter. Garnish with dill. Serve with French bread.

Shrimp in Pernod Cream Sauce

Makes 4 to 6 servings

3 cups water
1 to 2 teaspoons salt
⅛ teaspoon pepper
1 tablespoon anise seed
2 to 2½ pounds large shrimp,
　rinsed
⅓ cup sour cream
⅓ cup whipping cream
2 to 3 tablespoons Pernod
　Dash ground ginger
　Salt
　Chopped pistachios
　Lettuce leaves, washed and
　dried

In a stockpot or large saucepan, bring water, salt, pepper and anise seed to a boil. Add shrimp and simmer for about 6 minutes or until they are opaque. Do not overcook; drain and peel shrimp. Stir together sour cream and cream; add Pernod. Season to taste with ginger and salt. Pour sauce into a serving bowl and sprinkle with pistachios. Arrange shrimp on lettuce leaves. Serve sauce separately.

Lake Herring in Sherry
Makes about 6 servings

1½ pounds lake herring, ready
    to cook
    Juice of 1 lemon
    Salt
    White pepper
2 tablespoons flour
3 tablespoons butter
2 tablespoons cooking oil
1 cup water
3 tablespoons vinegar
2 onions, peeled and thinly
    sliced
1 carrot, scraped and thinly
    sliced
1 leek, trimmed, well-rinsed
    and thinly sliced
1 teaspoon mustard seed
½ teaspoon peppercorns
    Pinch of ground ginger,
    optional
    Salt
    Sugar
2 cups dry sherry
1 to 2 dried chili peppers

Rinse and dry fish. Sprinkle with lemon juice and marinate for 15 minutes. Pat dry and season to taste with salt and pepper. Dredge in flour. In a saucepan, heat butter and oil. Brown herring on both sides for 3 to 5 minutes. Drain on paper towels; cool. In a saucepan, heat water with next 7 ingredients. Add salt and sugar to taste; bring to a boil and simmer for about 15 minutes. Add sherry and chili peppers; simmer for 1 or 2 minutes. Place herring in a bowl, cover with hot marinade, and cool. Refrigerate for two days. May be served with potatoes or homemade bread.

Crab Meat with Mayonnaise
Makes 3 to 4 servings

10 to 12 ounces fresh-cooked
    crab meat
⅔ cup mayonnaise
2 to 3 tablespoons seafood
    cocktail sauce
    Lemon slices
    Fresh dill *or* parsley
    Toast points

Arrange crab meat in small serving bowls. Stir together mayonnaise and cocktail sauce and spoon over crab meat. Garnish with lemon slices and dill. Serve with toast points.
Variation: Use large shrimp instead of crab meat.

Island Breakfast
Makes 2 to 4 servings

½ cup sour cream
¼ cup whipping cream
1 teaspoon minced onion
Salt
Curry powder
Worcestershire sauce
2 to 3 tablespoons chopped dill and parsley
½ pound cooked shrimp, divided
4 hard-boiled eggs, peeled and halved
Watercress or parsley
Dark bread
Butter

In a small bowl, stir together sour cream, cream and onion; season to taste with salt, curry powder and Worcestershire sauce. Add chopped herbs and stir in half of the shrimp. Place in center of a serving dish and top with remaining shrimp. Place eggs around shrimp cream. Garnish with watercress or parsley. Serve with dark bread and butter.

Trout with Cucumber Mayonnaise
Makes 4 servings

1 quart water
2 tablespoons white wine vinegar
1½ teaspoons salt
6 crushed peppercorns
1 bay leaf
3 sprigs parsley
1 onion, peeled and chopped
1 celery rib, sliced
½ teaspoon dried thyme
4 small whole trout, ready to cook
½ cup mayonnaise
½ cup peeled and seeded cucumber, finely chopped
⅛ teaspoon dried dill
Pepper
Cucumber slices
Parsley
Cherry tomatoes

Combine first 9 ingredients in a sauté pan large enough to hold the trout. Bring to a boil and simmer, covered, for about 30 minutes. Add trout and poach for 5 minutes or until done. Drain and chill fish. Combine mayonnaise and cucumber in a small bowl. Stir in dill and season to taste with pepper. Place in center of a serving platter. Arrange trout and vegetables around mayonnaise.

Lobster Tails with Mustard Sauce
Makes 4 servings

⅔ cup mayonnaise
3 tablespoons hot mustard
  Salt, pepper, sugar
4 lobster tails, cooked and
  shelled
  Boston lettuce leaves,
  washed and dried
  Lemon wedges
  Parsley
  French bread
  Butter

In a small bowl, mix mayonnaise with mustard. Season to taste with salt, pepper and sugar. Arrange lobster tails on lettuce leaves placed on a serving platter or on four individual serving plates. Garnish with lemon wedges and parsley. Serve mustard sauce separately. Serve with French bread and butter.

Crispy Flounder Fillets
Makes 4 servings

⅔ cup flour
1 teaspoon dry yeast
½ teaspoon sugar
  Salt to taste
1 egg, lightly beaten
½ cup lukewarm water
¼ pound bacon, cut into fine
  strips
2 tablespoons almond slivers
4 flounder fillets, about
  ¾ pound each
  Lemon juice
  Salt
  Pepper
  Vegetable oil
  Sauce Remoulade (see page
  166)
  Lettuce leaves, washed and
  dried
  Cooked crumbled bacon
  Blanched almond slices,
  toasted
  Lemon slices

Sift flour into a medium bowl; mix with yeast. Add sugar, salt, egg and water. Beat with electric hand mixer, first on low, then on high, for a total of 5 minutes. Stir in bacon strips and almond slivers. Cover bowl and set in a warm place to rise. When double in bulk, stir vigorously. Rinse fillets and pat dry. Sprinkle with lemon juice and set aside for 15 minutes; pat dry. Season to taste with salt and pepper; dip in batter. In an electric skillet, heat about 1½ inches of oil to 375° F. Add fillets; fry for 5 minutes or until light brown. Drain on paper towels; cool. Prepare Sauce Remoulade. Line a platter with lettuce leaves, place sauce in center and surround with fillets. Sprinkle with bacon or almonds, or both. Garnish with lemon slices.

Marinated Trout

Makes 4 servings

4 trout fillets
Fresh dill, coarsely chopped
1 tablespoon salt
4 tablespoons sugar, divided
2 tablespoons white pepper
1 teaspoon brandy, optional
4 tablespoons hot mustard
1 teaspoon dry mustard
2 tablespoons wine vinegar
5 tablespoons vegetable oil
3 tablespoons chopped dill *or*
   2 teaspoons dried dill

Rinse fillets and pat dry. Place two of the fillets in a shallow bowl, skin side down. Sprinkle with dill. Mix salt, 1 tablespoon of the sugar and pepper; sprinkle over trout. Add brandy; top with remaining 2 fillets, skin side up. Cover trout with foil. Place a board or heavy cardboard, longer than the trout, over foil and weight with something heavy. Refrigerate for 2 or 3 days. Baste occasionally with the accumulated juices. In a small bowl, combine mustard, dry mustard, remaining 3 tablespoons sugar and vinegar; mix well. Gradually whisk in oil; add dill. Remove trout from marinade. Blot dry and skin. Arrange on a serving platter. Serve sauce separately.

Pickled Herring in Herb Sauce

Makes 4 to 8 servings

8 pickled herring fillets
Club soda
3 onions, peeled
½ small cucumber, peeled
2 medium apples, peeled,
   quartered and cored
1 cup sour cream
⅓ cup whipping cream
2 tablespoons wine vinegar
2 tablespoons white wine
Salt
Pepper
2 tablespoons chopped chives
1 tablespoon chopped fresh
   dill *or* ¼ teaspoon dried dill

Soak herring in a little club soda for 1 to 2 hours. Chop onions, cucumber and apples. In a medium bowl combine sour cream, cream, vinegar and wine; add vegetables and apples. Season to taste with salt and pepper. Stir in chives and dill. Pat herring fillets dry. Dip both sides in sauce. Place sauce on a serving plate and arrange herring on top.

Marinated Trout, this page

100

Poached Brook Trout
Makes 4 servings

1 cup water
1 cup dry white wine *or*
   vermouth
1 lemon slice
½ onion, peeled and sliced
3 sprigs parsley
½ bay leaf
½ carrot
1 to 2 teaspoons salt
3 crushed peppercorns
4 frozen brook trout, thawed
   Parsley
   Lemon slices
   Green Sauce (see page 165)

In a large skillet, combine first 9 ingredients. Bring to a boil; reduce heat and simmer, covered, for about 10 minutes. Add trout; return to boil, then simmer, covered, until fish flakes (about 6 to 10 minutes). Remove from heat; cool and refrigerate trout in liquid for several hours. Remove trout to a serving platter. Garnish with parsley and lemon slices. Serve with Green Sauce.

Marinated Eel
Makes 5 to 6 servings

1½ pounds ready-to-cook eel,
   skinned
   Juice of ½ lemon
1 cup vinegar
2 cups dry white wine
1 cup water
4 onions, peeled and sliced
2 carrots, scraped and sliced
½ leek, sliced and rinsed, green
   discarded
2 tablespoons chopped parsley
1 teaspoon white peppercorns
2 cloves
1 teaspoon mustard seed
5 dried chili peppers
1½ teaspoons salt
2 tablespoons olive oil
   French bread
   Butter

Rinse eel, pat dry and cut into serving-sized pieces. Sprinkle with lemon juice; marinate for 15 minutes. In a stockpot, combine all other ingredients, except the oil. Bring to a boil and simmer for about 20 minutes. Add eel and simmer for 20 to 25 minutes more. Let cool in liquid. If needed, add more salt and vinegar. Stir in oil. Refrigerate for 1 to 2 days. Serve with French bread and butter.

Smoked Fish on Potato Salad

Makes about 4 servings

½ pound boiled potatoes,
  still hot
½ pound small peas, cooked
  and drained
2 ounces cooked *or* canned
  mushrooms, drained
3 tablespoons mayonnaise
2 tablespoons sour cream
2 tablespoons whipping cream
  Salt
  Pepper
  Vinegar
1¼ pounds smoked fish fillets,
  skinned
  Tomato wedges
  Parsley

Peel potatoes while still hot; cool and dice. Combine with peas and mushrooms in a non-metallic bowl. In a small bowl, stir together mayonnaise, sour cream and cream. Season to taste with salt, pepper and vinegar. Pour over vegetables; mix well and set aside for 30 minutes. Arrange potato salad in a serving bowl; top with smoked fish. Garnish with tomato wedges and parsley.

Lobster Salad

Makes 3 to 4 servings

1 small orange, peeled and
  sectioned
1 cup cooked diced lobster
  meat
⅔ cup cooked diced shrimp
½ cup shredded Bibb lettuce
1 teaspoon minced dill *or*
  parsley
⅔ cup mayonnaise
2 tablespoons sour cream
1 tablespoon seafood cocktail
  sauce
  Salt
  Pepper
  Lemon juice
  Lettuce leaves, washed and
  dried

Remove orange sections from their membrane. Dice pulp and combine in a bowl with next four ingredients. In a small bowl, combine mayonnaise with sour cream and cocktail sauce. Season to taste with salt, pepper and lemon juice. Fold into salad ingredients. Line serving dish with lettuce leaves. Arrange salad on top.

Mixed Seafood Platter

Makes 4 to 8 servings

**Boston lettuce leaves,
washed and dried
Lemon juice**
½ **pound cooked shrimp**
4 **pickled herring fillets**
4 **tablespoons Horseradish
Cream (see page 166)**
4 **small smoked trout fillets,
skinned and halved**
4 **slices smoked salmon,
halved and rolled up**
Lemon slices *or* **wedges**
Dill *or* **parsley**

Arrange lettuce leaves on serving platter; sprinkle with lemon juice. Place shrimp in center. Roll up herring fillets, leaving a hollow in center; fill hollow with Horseradish Cream. Cut rolls in half. Arrange with remaining seafood around shrimp. Garnish with lemon slices and dill.

Pickled Herring in Cream Sauce

Makes 4 to 8 servings

1½ **cups whipping cream**
3 **to 4 tablespoons white wine
vinegar**
¼ **teaspoon mustard seed**
4 **peppercorns**
1 **bay leaf**
4 **onions, peeled and sliced**
2 **medium dill pickles, sliced**
8 **pickled herring fillets**
French bread
Butter

In a salad bowl, mix cream, vinegar, mustard seed and peppercorns. Add bay leaf, onions and pickles. Marinate herring fillets in cream sauce for 24 hours. Serve with French bread and butter.

*Pickled Herring in Cream
Sauce, this page*

Dilled Shrimp
Makes 8 servings

½ cup mayonnaise
1 8-ounce package Neufchatel cheese, softened
¼ pound cooked shrimp
1 teaspoon lemon juice
1 teaspoon Worcestershire sauce
2 tablespoons minced parsley
½ teaspoon minced garlic
¼ teaspoon minced dill

Combine mayonnaise and cheese in a blender or food processor. Stir in remaining ingredients. Cover and chill well before serving.

Prawns with Salsa Picante
Makes 10 servings

1 pound medium prawns *or* shrimp (24 to 26 per pound)
1 to 1½ cups wine
1 clove garlic, minced
1 lemon, sliced
4 sprigs cilantro *or* parsley
Salt and pepper to taste
1 large apple
Bottled picante sauce

In a large saucepan, cover prawns with wine and enough boiling water to cover. Add garlic, lemon, cilantro, salt and pepper. Cook over medium heat 3 to 5 minutes or until pink. Drain, shell, and devein shrimp. Skewer shrimp with wooden picks. Spear the apple with the picks so that the shrimp are displayed in a fan-like arrangement. Serve with picante sauce.

Flounder Fillets on Toast
Makes 4 servings

½ cup mayonnaise
1 tablespoon ketchup
1 tablespoon minced chives
12 to 14 ounces flounder fillets
Lemon juice
Salt
Pepper
Flour
Vegetable oil
4 slices toast

In a small bowl, mix mayonnaise, ketchup and chives. Rinse fish; pat dry. Cut into 2-inch pieces; place in a shallow dish. Sprinkle with lemon juice; set aside for 15 minutes. Pat dry. Sprinkle with salt and pepper to taste; dredge in flour. In an electric skillet, heat about 1 inch of oil to 375° F. Fry fish, submerged, in batches for 3 minutes or until lightly brown. Drain on paper towels. Serve hot or let cool. Arrange fillet pieces on toast; top with mayonnaise.

Carp in Vinaigrette

Makes about 6 servings

1 ready-to-cook carp, about
   3½ pounds
Salt
Pepper
Vegetable oil
Vinaigrette Sauce (recipe
   below)
Parsley
Tomato wedges
Egg slices
Lemon slices

Preheat oven to 450° F. Rinse carp and blot dry. Season inside and out with salt and pepper. Brush a piece of heavy-duty foil large enough to hold the fish with oil. Wrap fish loosely and seal seams firmly. Place on a baking sheet and bake for 50 to 60 minutes. Unwrap and place on serving platter to cool. Sprinkle cold carp with a little vinaigrette; serve remaining sauce separately. Garnish platter with parsley, tomato wedges, egg and lemon slices. May be served with white bread, toast or parslied potatoes.

Vinaigrette Sauce

1 cup vegetable oil
2 tablespoons vinegar
1 hard-boiled egg, peeled and
   chopped
1½ tablespoons chopped parsley
1 teaspoon chopped chives
1 tablespoon chopped basil
   leaves *or* ½ teaspoon dried
   basil
Salt
Pepper

In a small bowl, whisk together oil and vinegar. Stir in remaining ingredients and season to taste with salt and pepper.

Gourmet Smoked Salmon Rolls

Makes about 4 servings

2 to 3 tablespoons mayonnaise
8 even slices smoked salmon
2 hard-boiled eggs, peeled and
   quartered
   Boston lettuce leaves,
   washed and dried
Parsley

Spread mayonnaise over ¼ of each slice of smoked salmon. Place egg wedges on top of mayonnaise and roll up smoked salmon. Arrange on lettuce leaves. Garnish with parsley. Serve with toast points and butter.

Salmon Steaks in Tartar Sauce
Makes 4 servings

4 salmon steaks, about
6 ounces each
Lemon juice
Salt
Pepper
Butter
3 tablespoons mayonnaise
3 tablespoons sour cream
2 hard-boiled eggs, peeled and chopped
1 tablespoon chopped chives
1 to 2 teaspoons chopped parsley
1 teaspoon chopped dill
Boston lettuce leaves, washed and dried
Tomato wedges
Parsley

Rinse salmon and pat dry. Sprinkle with lemon juice and marinate for 15 minutes. Season with salt and pepper to taste. Preheat oven to 450° F. Butter 4 pieces of foil large enough to hold the steaks. Wrap each steak loosely and seal seam tightly; bake for 25 to 30 minutes. Open foil and let salmon cool; brush with melted butter. In a small bowl, combine mayonnaise and sour cream. Stir in eggs and herbs. Season to taste with salt and pepper. Arrange salmon on a plate lined with lettuce leaves. Garnish with tomato wedges and parsley. Serve sauce separately.

Marinated Shrimp and Artichoke Hearts
Makes 4 dozen

1 10-ounce package frozen artichoke hearts
24 medium shrimp
1 large egg yolk
½ cup olive oil
½ cup peanut oil
¼ cup wine vinegar
2 tablespoons Dijon-style mustard
2 tablespoons minced fresh parsley
2 tablespoons minced fresh chives
1 tablespoon minced shallots
Bibb lettuce leaves
Watercress sprigs

Cook artichoke hearts according to package directions. Drain and refrigerate. Cook shrimp in boiling salted water until just pink. Drain and cool about 10 minutes, until cool enough to handle; peel and devein. Beat egg yolk in medium mixing bowl. Add oils, vinegar and mustard; beat well. Add parsley, chives, shallots, artichoke hearts and shrimp. Stir gently to mix. Marinate 2 hours at room temperature. Drain and serve with wooden picks, or place small portions of drained mixture on bibb lettuce leaves and garnish with watercress sprigs, if desired.

Salmon Steaks in Tartar Sauce, this page

Salmon and Ginger Cream

Makes 4 servings

4 salmon steaks
1 cup Gewurztraminer wine *or*
    any chablis
1 lemon, thinly sliced
1 onion, thinly sliced
6 whole peppercorns
3 or 4 parsley sprigs
4 ounces Neufchatel cheese,
    softened
¼ cup plain yogurt
2 teaspoons grated ginger root
    or chopped candied ginger
    Grated peel of 1 lemon

Preheat oven to 350° F. Place salmon steaks in an ovenproof baking dish. Pour wine over steaks. Top with lemon, onion, peppercorns, and parsley sprigs. Cover and poach in oven for 15 minutes. In a bowl, combine cheese, yogurt, ginger root, and lemon peel; blend well. Serve at room temperature or chilled over cold salmon.

Potted Shrimp

Makes 6 servings

10 to 12 ounces shrimp, cooked
    and peeled
3 tablespoons sherry,
    medium dry
3 tablespoons lemon juice
    Peel of 1 lemon
2 tablespoons minced dill
    Pepper
¾ cup butter, melted

Marinate shrimp, covered, for 1 hour in sherry, lemon juice, peel, dill, and pepper to taste. Remove lemon peel. Spoon shrimp mixture into 6 custard cups; press lightly. Pour melted butter over shrimp; set aside until firm.

Smoked Salmon with Horseradish Cream

Makes 5 to 10 servings

1 cup whipping cream
4 to 5 tablespoons horseradish
    Lemon juice
    Salt
    Sugar
10 slices smoked salmon
    Fresh dill

Whip cream until stiff, fold in horseradish and season to taste with lemon juice, salt and sugar. Reserve a small amount. Twist smoked salmon slices into cones. Fit a pastry bag with a star tip. Spoon horseradish cream into bag and pipe into cones. Arrange cones on a platter and garnish with dill. Serve with remaining cream.

Marinated Mackerel

Makes 4 to 5 servings

2 pounds mackerel, skinned
  and filleted
2 to 3 red onions, peeled and
  sliced
½ cup vinegar
1 cup water
10 to 15 peppercorns
2 to 3 bay leaves
4 to 5 juniper berries
1 teaspoon salt
1 tablespoon sugar
  Dill, finely chopped

Rinse fish and pat dry. Place in a non-metallic bowl together with onion slices separated into rings. In a medium saucepan, combine vinegar and water with remaining ingredients, except dill; bring to a boil and simmer for five minutes. Cool and pour over fish; cover and chill for 2 days. Sprinkle fish with dill before serving. Goes well with pumpernickel and butter.

Smoked Trout

Makes 4 servings

8 to 12 romaine *or* Belgian
  endive leaves, washed and
  dried
1 orange, sliced crosswise
2 smoked trout
  Lemon juice
4 teaspoons horseradish
4 tablespoons sour cream
1 to 2 tablespoons minced dill
  Salt
  Pepper
  Lemon juice

Arrange lettuce leaves and orange slices on 4 serving plates. Fillet and skin trout. Place one fillet each on top of lettuce; sprinkle with lemon juice. Put one teaspoon horseradish next to each fillet. Mix sour cream and dill. Season to taste with remaining ingredients. Spoon over trout.

Helpful Hints

3 ounces of dried mushrooms after soaking equal 1 pound of fresh mushrooms.

When doubling a recipe do not double seasonings before tasting.

Meat

Stuffed Beef

(Illustrated previous page)
Makes 4 to 5 servings

2 pounds trimmed fillet of
   beef, center cut
4 tablespoons vegetable oil,
   divided
1 onion, peeled and minced
2 cloves garlic, peeled and
   minced, divided
2 tablespoons pine nuts,
   lightly toasted and ground
4 tablespoons whipping
   cream, divided
   Salt
   Pepper
6 tablespoons chopped mixed
   herbs, divided
4 ounces Gorgonzola
½ cup sour cream
   Cherry tomatoes
   Parsley *or* watercress

Rinse meat and pat dry. Heat 1 tablespoon of the oil in a small skillet. Add onion and ½ of the garlic; sauté until limp. Remove from heat; stir in ground nuts and 1 tablespoon of the whipping cream. Season to taste with salt and pepper. Add 3 tablespoons of the herbs. Make a deep cut the length of the meat. Place onion and herb filling in the cut. Close and tie meat in 2-inch intervals with kitchen string. Place meat in a roasting pan. Stir remaining garlic with remaining 3 tablespoons oil. Add salt and pepper to taste; stir in herbs. Spread over meat. Cover pan and set aside for 2 hours. Preheat oven to 425° F. Uncover roasting pan. Roast meat for 35 to 40 minutes, turning it 2 or 3 times during roasting. Let meat cool completely; remove string. Mash cheese with a fork, or force through a sieve. Mix with remaining 3 tablespoons of whipping cream and sour cream. For a very smooth sauce, briefly beat ingredients with an electric hand-mixer. To serve, slice meat and arrange slices on a platter. Garnish with cherry tomatoes and parsley or watercress. Serve Gorgonzola sauce separately.

Barbecued Spareribs

Makes 8 to 10 servings

½ cup brown sugar
1 cup ketchup
¼ cup soy sauce
¼ teaspoon cumin
2 tablespoons sherry
2 tablespoons vinegar
2 pounds spareribs

Combine all ingredients except spareribs, mixing well. Marinate ribs 3 to 4 hours in sauce. Remove from sauce and bake, covered, in a 300° F. oven for 1½ hours. Remove cover, add sauce; bake 1 hour longer, basting occasionally. Cool.

Spring Platter with Avocado Cream
Makes about 5 servings

2 pounds boneless pork loin
  roast
Salt
Pepper
2 medium leeks, trimmed and
  washed
2 fennel bulbs, trimmed and
  washed
2 large carrots
4 celery ribs, trimmed and
  strings removed
4 to 6 small tomatoes
¼ cup vegetable oil
2 tablespoons herbed vinegar
Salt
Pepper
Sugar
Parsley
Avocado Cream (recipe
  below)

Preheat oven to 350° F. Rinse meat and pat dry. Trim excess fat; rub with salt and pepper. Place on a rack in an open roasting pan; insert meat thermometer. Roast for 1½ to 2 hours or until thermometer registers 170° F. Remove from oven; cool. Remove green parts from leeks to within 3 inches of stalks. Cut in half lengthwise; rinse well. Cut fennel bulbs into wedges. Scrape carrot; quarter lengthwise. Cut celery, leek and carrot into 3-inch lengths. In boiling salted water, cook celery for about 2 minutes, leek for 2 to 3 minutes, fennel for about 8 minutes, and carrot for 5 minutes. Turn off heat and dip tomatoes in the hot liquid for 15 to 20 seconds. Plunge in cold water and peel. Drain all vegetables well. Place in a shallow non-metallic container. In a small bowl, whisk oil and vinegar; season to taste with salt, pepper and sugar. Pour over vegetables and marinate for 2 to 3 hours. Baste with marinade occasionally. Drain. Shortly before serving, slice meat thinly and arrange on a large platter with the marinated vegetables. Garnish with parsley. Serve Avocado Cream separately.

Avocado Cream
Makes about ⅔ cup

1 ripe avocado
1 to 1½ tablespoons lemon
  juice, divided
1 garlic clove, crushed
¼ cup vegetable oil
Pepper
Onion salt
Parsley

Peel, halve and pit avocado. In a small bowl, mash pulp with a fork and stir in 1 tablespoon of lemon juice and the garlic. Stir in oil by the tablespoonful. Season to taste with pepper, onion salt and lemon juice. Transfer to a serving bowl and garnish with parsley. Prepare just before serving.

Greek Meat Loaf
Makes about 6 servings

2 hard rolls
1 tablespoon vegetable oil
¼ pound slab bacon, cubed
2 onions, peeled and diced
2 cloves garlic, peeled and
  crushed
2 pounds ground beef
3 eggs
2 tablespoons chopped parsley
2 tablespoons chopped chives
1 tablespoon tomato paste
  Salt
  Pepper
  Paprika
6 ounces Feta cheese
6 tablespoons whipping cream
  Thyme
  Basil
3 bay leaves
1 to 2 tablespoons pine nuts
  Tomato Sauce (recipe below)

Soak rolls in cold water; squeeze. Tear into small pieces. Heat oil in a skillet. Add bacon cubes and cook until crisp. Add onion and garlic; sauté until transparent. Let cool. Mix with rolls, ground beef, eggs, parsley, chives and tomato paste. Season to taste with salt, pepper and paprika. In a separate bowl, mash cheese with a fork. Stir with cream and season to taste with thyme and basil. Preheat oven to 375° F. Brush a deep 10-inch pie plate or a shallow ovenproof soufflé dish with vegetable oil. Add half the beef in an even layer. Top with cheese and remaining beef; spread evenly. Lightly sprinkle with vegetable oil. Bake for about 40 minutes. Place bay leaves on top of loaf and sprinkle with pine nuts. Bake for 20 to 30 minutes more. Serve hot or cold with Tomato Sauce.

Tomato Sauce

2 onions, peeled and minced
2 cloves garlic, peeled and
  minced
1 16-ounce can stewed
  tomatoes
3 tablespoons red wine vinegar
1 teaspoon Dijon-style
  mustard
1 tablespoon sugar
1 teaspoon ground cinnamon,
  optional
  Chili powder
  Salt
  Pepper

In a large saucepan, combine onion, garlic, tomatoes and vinegar. Bring to a boil and simmer for 15 minutes. Strain through a sieve. Return to saucepan. Stir in mustard, sugar and cinnamon. Simmer for about 30 minutes or until sauce starts to thicken. Season to taste with chili powder, salt and pepper.

Pork and Almond Medallions

Makes about 4 servings

1 pork tenderloin, about 1½
   pounds
   Salt
   Pepper
1 to 2 eggs, lightly beaten
3 ounces sliced blanched almonds
1 tablespoon vegetable oil
2 tablespoons margarine
3 tablespoons mayonnaise
2 tablespoons whipping cream
2 tablespoons sour cream
2 tomatoes, peeled, halved,
   seeded and diced
1 dill pickle, diced
1 teaspoon crushed green
   peppercorns
1 tablespoon chopped fresh
   dill *or* ¼ teaspoon dried dill
   Watercress

Rinse tenderloin; pat dry. Cut into slices about ⅔ inch thick. Season with salt and pepper to taste. Dip both sides in egg, then in almond slices. Press almonds firmly into meat. Heat oil and margarine in a skillet. Brown medallions and fry for 5 to 7 minutes on each side. Let cool. In a small serving bowl, mix mayonnaise with cream and sour cream. Add remaining ingredients; correct seasoning with pepper. Arrange medallions on a serving platter. Garnish with watercress. Serve mayonnaise separately.

Sweet and Sour Pork Tenderloin

Makes about 3 servings

1 pork tenderloin, about 1
   pound
   Salt
   Pepper
   Garlic powder
1 slice bacon
   Bottled sweet and sour sauce
1½ tablespoons hot water

Preheat oven to 325° F. Rinse meat; pat dry. Place meat on a rack in roasting pan. Season to taste with salt, pepper, and garlic powder. Put bacon along top of tenderloin. Roast for 40 minutes; remove bacon. Brush generously with sweet and sour sauce; roast for another 30 to 35 minutes, brushing with sauce occasionally. Remove from oven; cool and refrigerate. Slice meat and arrange on a serving platter. Mix well 1½ tablespoons sweet and sour sauce and hot water; brush lightly over meat slices.

Syrian-Style Meatballs
Makes about 8 servings

1½ pounds ground lamb
5 cooked carrots, puréed
1 to 2 cloves garlic, peeled and crushed
2 cups cooked rice
2 eggs
Salt
Pepper
Curry powder
⅔ cup sesame seed
Vegetable oil
⅓ cup sour cream
⅓ cup whipping cream
⅔ cup yogurt

In a medium bowl, combine lamb with next 4 ingredients. Add salt, pepper and curry powder to taste. Mix well. Form about 45 walnut-sized balls. Roll half the balls in sesame seeds. In an electric skillet, heat 1 to 1½ inches of oil to 375° F. Fry meatballs in batches for about 5 minutes. Drain on paper towels. In a small bowl, combine sour cream, cream and yogurt. Season to taste with salt and pepper. Serve meatballs hot or cold. Serve yogurt cream separately.

Boiled Beef and Vegetables
Makes 4 to 5 servings

2 pounds trimmed beef brisket, round roast *or* boneless rump roast
2 tablespoons olive oil
Salt
Pepper
5 sprigs parsley
3 onions, peeled and halved
1 clove garlic, peeled and halved
1 cup red wine
1½ quarts beef stock
1 to 2 bay leaves
Thyme
4 to 6 carrots, scraped
2 small zucchini, sliced
8 ounces green beans, trimmed
1 small cabbage, trimmed, quartered and cored
Chopped parsley
Green Sauce (see page 165)

Rinse beef; pat dry. Heat oil in a dutch oven and brown meat on all sides. Season to taste with salt and pepper. Add parsley, onion and garlic; sauté briefly until limp. Add wine, stock, bay leaves and thyme to taste. Bring to a boil, then simmer gently for 1½ to 2 hours or until meat is tender. Remove meat and let cool. Strain broth. In a large saucepan, bring broth to a boil. Add carrots and cook for about 8 minutes; remove. Cook zucchini for about 2 minutes, beans for 8 to 10 minutes, and cabbage wedges for about 10 minutes. Drain vegetables well. Slice meat and arrange on a serving platter. Add vegetables. Sprinkle vegetables with parsley. Serve with Green Sauce.

Variation: Instead of vegetables, add pickles, pickled watermelon rind and whole cranberry sauce to meat platter. Serve with Horseradish Cream instead of Green Sauce.

Syrian-Style Meatballs, this page

Stuffed Pork Chops
Makes 4 servings

3 precooked bratwurst
   sausages, skinned
⅓ cup whipping cream
¼ cup parsley leaves
   Grated rind of ½ lemon
1 teaspoon capers *or* 1 teaspoon green peppercorns
2 slices white bread
4 thick pork loin chops
   Salt
   Pepper
2 tablespoons shortening *or* oil
   Watercress
   Lemon slices

Cut sausages into small pieces. Combine in food processor with cream, parsley, lemon rind and capers. Process with the steel knife until just blended. Remove to a medium bowl. Tear bread into small pieces and add to stuffing. Preheat oven to 350° F. Cut pockets in the chops from the fat side. Divide stuffing among the pockets. Close openings with toothpicks. Season chops with salt and pepper. Heat the shortening in an ovenproof skillet large enough to hold the chops. Brown chops for about 3 minutes on each side. Cover skillet and place in oven for about 35 minutes. Remove cover and bake for another 25 to 30 minutes. Transfer chops to a serving platter and let cool. Garnish with watercress and lemon slices.

Lamb Chops Persillade
Makes 4 servings

4 lamb loin chops, cut ¾ to 1
   inch thick
2 cloves garlic, minced
1 tablespoon butter
3 tablespoons finely minced
   shallots *or* green onion
⅓ cup fine bread crumbs
⅓ cup minced fresh parsley
1 teaspoon tarragon, basil, *or*
   thyme
   Freshly ground pepper
   Grated Parmesan cheese

Line the broiler pan with foil to collect drippings. Sprinkle chops with garlic; place in pan. Broil 4 inches from heat source for 6 to 8 minutes on each side. Cool to room temperature. Melt butter in a saucepan; sauté shallots and bread crumbs until golden brown. Remove from heat. Stir in parsley, herbs, and drippings from lamb chops. Add pepper and cheese to taste. Spread over one side of chops just before serving.

Fruit-Stuffed Pork Loin
Makes about 8 servings

1 cup water
½ cup Madeira *or* sherry
1 stick cinnamon
3 cloves
1 pound mixed dried fruit
   (prunes, apricots, apples)
3½ to 4 pounds boneless pork
   loin roast
   Salt
   Pepper
   Paprika

In a large saucepan, bring water, wine, cinnamon and cloves to a boil; add fruit. Simmer for 10 to 15 minutes. Let cool in liquid. Drain. Rinse meat; pat dry. With a thin-bladed knife, cut a cylindrical piece, about 2 inches in diameter, from the center of the loin not quite to the other end. Reserve meat cylinder for another use. Rub roast with salt, pepper and paprika to taste. Fill cavity with stewed fruit; close with a piece of foil. Preheat oven to 400° F. Place roast on a large piece of heavy-duty foil. Wrap loosely; seal tightly. Roast for 1¾ to 2 hours. Remove from oven. Let rest, wrapped, for about 10 minutes. Open foil; let meat cool. Slice meat and arrange on a platter.

Veal Rolls Clarissa
Makes about 4 servings

2 tablespoons dried wild
   mushrooms, preferably cépes
½ cup water
3 tablespoons fine bread
   crumbs
1 egg
¼ pound ground ham
2 tablespoons chopped parsley
   Basil
   Salt
   Pepper
8 thin, long veal scallops,
   about 3 ounces each
   Prepared mustard
3 tablespoons olive oil
½ cup white wine
   Tomato wedges
   Parsley

Soak mushrooms in water for about 12 hours. Drain, reserving liquid; dice. In a small bowl, combine reserved liquid, mushrooms and next 4 ingredients. Season to taste with basil, salt and pepper. Spread one side of scallops thinly with mustard. Cover with mushroom filling. Roll up and tie with string. Heat oil in a skillet. Add veal rolls and brown on all sides for about 10 minutes. Add wine; reduce heat and simmer, covered, for about 15 minutes, turning once. Remove from pan; let cool. Remove string. Slice rolls thickly. Arrange slices, overlapping, on a platter. Degrease pan juices; pour juices over meat. Garnish with tomato wedges and parsley.

Boneless Pork Loin with Fruit

Makes 6 servings

1 3-pound boneless pork loin
  roast
  Ground ginger
6 cloves
1 tablespoon shortening
6 canned lychees, drained
6 canned peach halves,
  drained
⅔ to 1 cup canned sour cherries, drained
2 teaspoons Kirsch or brandy
6 canned pear halves, drained
1 to 2 tablespoons shredded
  coconut

Preheat oven to 350° F. Rinse meat; pat dry. Rub meat with ginger to taste; stud with cloves. Place in a casserole; melt shortening and pour over meat. Roast, uncovered, for 2 to 2½ hours or until done. Baste occasionally with accumulated pan juices. Remove from oven; let cool. Place lychees in peach cavities. In a small bowl, sprinkle cherries with kirsch or brandy; mix and spoon into pear cavities. Slice meat; arrange on a serving platter together with fruit. Sprinkle fruit with coconut. May be served with French or Italian bread.

Meatballs with Roquefort Stuffing

Makes 4 servings

1 hard roll
1 tablespoon vegetable oil
1 onion, peeled and minced
1 clove garlic, peeled and
  minced
1 pound ground beef
2 eggs
2 tablespoons ketchup
2 tablespoons parsley, chopped
  Salt
  Pepper
¼ pound Roquefort or Gor-
  gonzola cheese
3 tablespoons finely ground
  bread crumbs
  Vegetable oil

Soak roll in cold water. Squeeze; tear into small pieces. In a small skillet, heat 1 tablespoon oil. Add onion and garlic; sauté until limp. Remove from heat. Combine with roll, ground beef, eggs, ketchup and parsley. Season to taste with salt and pepper. Form about 22 walnut-sized balls. Cut cheese into small pieces. With the handle of a wooden spoon, make a deep indentation in each meatball. Insert a piece of cheese; reshape balls. Roll in bread crumbs. In an electric skillet, heat 1 to 1½ inches of oil to 375° F. Add meatballs in batches; fry for about 5 minutes. Drain on paper towels. Serve hot or cold.

Pork Chops with Mustard

Makes 4 servings

4 pork loin chops, 6 to
   8 ounces each
Salt
Pepper
Prepared mustard
4 onions, peeled and minced
2 cloves garlic, peeled and
   minced
3 to 4 tablespoons vege-
   table oil
⅓ cup sour cream
⅓ cup whipping cream
1½ to 2 teaspoons Dijon-style
   mustard
Curry powder
Parsley

Preheat oven to 350° F. Rinse chops and pat dry. Season to taste with salt and pepper. Thinly spread with mustard. Top chops with onion and garlic. Brush a roasting pan with oil. Add the chops and bake, covered, for about 30 minutes. Remove cover and bake for another 20 to 25 minutes, or until chops are tender. Keep warm or let cool. In a small bowl, combine sour cream and cream; add mustard and curry powder to taste. Arrange chops on a serving platter. Garnish with parsley. Serve mustard sauce separately.

Pork Tenderloin with Mayonnaise

Makes about 4 servings

1½ pounds trimmed, whole
   pork tenderloin
Salt
Pepper
Marjoram
4 slices bacon
Parsley
Tomato wedges
⅔ cup mayonnaise
2 tablespoons yogurt *or* sour
   cream
2 medium tomatoes, peeled,
   seeded and chopped
1 medium dill pickle, chopped
1 tablespoon chopped mixed
   herbs

Preheat oven to 400° F. Rinse meat and pat dry. Season lightly with salt and pepper; add marjoram to taste. Wrap in bacon slices. Place in a casserole and roast, uncovered, for 30 to 35 minutes. Remove bacon. Let meat cool. Slice meat and arrange on a platter. Garnish with parsley and tomato wedges. In a small serving bowl, combine mayonnaise with remaining ingredients. Correct seasoning with salt and pepper. Serve separately.

Saltimbocca

Makes 4 servings

3 tablespoons olive oil
8 veal scallops, about 3
  ounces each
Salt
Pepper
8 slices prosciutto ham,
  trimmed to fit veal scallops
16 fresh sage leaves
½ cup white wine
French bread
Marinated tomatoes

Heat oil in a skillet and lightly brown scallops for 2 minutes on each side. Season to taste with salt and pepper. Remove from pan. In the same skillet, heat ham very briefly on both sides. Remove. Add the sage to the pan and wilt. Remove from heat. Place 1 sage leaf on each scallop; top with a ham slice and fold over. Place remaining sage leaves on top; secure with toothpicks. Return skillet to heat. Add wine and deglaze pan. Pour juices over scallops. Serve warm or cold. Serve with French bread and tomatoes marinated in your choice of dressing.

Tenderloin Braids Madagascar

Makes 4 servings

4 small, slim pork tenderloins,
  about ½ pound each
Salt
Pepper
Paprika
1 tablespoon vegetable oil
1 tablespoon margarine
⅓ cup sour cream
⅓ cup whipping cream
3 tablespoons ketchup
1 teaspoon crushed green
  peppercorns
Chili powder
Parsley

Rinse meat; pat dry. Starting 1½ inches from thick end of tenderloins, cut the meat into 3 even strips, still connected at the thick end. Braid tenderloins; secure ends with toothpicks. Season to taste with salt, pepper and paprika. Heat oil and margarine in a skillet large enough to hold braids. Brown meat on all sides and fry for about 30 minutes; let cool. In a small serving bowl, combine sour cream, cream, ketchup and green peppercorns. Season to taste with salt and chili powder. Arrange braided tenderloins on a serving platter. Garnish with parsley. Serve sauce separately.

Saltimbocca, this page

Veal Roast Provencale

Makes 8 to 10 servings

1 rolled veal rump *or* shoulder
  roast, 4 to 5 pounds
Salt
White pepper
Marjoram
2 cloves garlic, peeled and
  crushed
¼ pound very thinly sliced
  bacon
Wine Aspic (see page 68)
Vegetables Provencale (recipe
  below)
Parsley

Preheat oven to 400° F. Rinse meat and pat dry. Season to taste with salt, pepper and marjoram. Spread garlic over meat. Place about half the bacon slices side by side on a large piece of heavy-duty foil. Put roast on bacon; cover with remaining slices. Wrap loosely and seal tightly. Roast for about 2¼ hours. Remove from oven. Let rest in foil for about 10 minutes. Open foil; let roast cool. Slice meat and arrange on a serving platter. May be glazed with Wine Aspic (see page 68). Garnish with Vegetables Provencale and parsley.

Vegetables Provencale

2 pounds spinach, trimmed
  and washed
3 to 4 cloves garlic, minced
  and divided
4 tablespoons olive oil,
  divided
Lemon juice
Salt, pepper and sugar
4 to 5 meaty tomatoes, about
  2 pounds
3 tablespoons chopped parsley
2 to 3 tablespoons pine nuts

Place wet spinach in a large saucepan or stockpot. Cover and steam over medium heat for 3 to 4 minutes. Chop coarsely. In a medium bowl, stir 1 to 2 cloves garlic into 3 tablespoons olive oil. Mix with the spinach. Season to taste with lemon juice, salt, pepper and sugar. Press into 8 to 10 small cups or custard cups. Set aside. Preheat oven to 400° F. Cut tomatoes in half; arrange in one layer in a shallow buttered baking dish. Sprinkle with salt and pepper. Sprinkle remaining 2 cloves garlic over tomatoes. Add parsley and pine nuts; sprinkle with remaining olive oil. Bake for about 25 minutes. Let cool. Unmold spinach; place around meat platter alternately with tomatoes.

Turkish Marinated Lamb

Makes about 8 servings

3½ pounds boneless leg of
    lamb, trimmed
3 onions, peeled and minced
5 to 6 cloves garlic, peeled and
    crushed, divided
⅔ cup olive oil, divided
5 to 6 tablespoons lemon
    juice, divided
2 teaspoons dried thyme
    Salt
    White pepper
    Vegetable oil
¼ cup water
¼ cup dry white wine
    Sugar
2 pounds firm tomatoes,
    halved, cored and seeded
    Tarragon
⅓ cup sour cream
⅓ cup whipping cream
⅔ cup yogurt
    Pita bread

Rinse meat and pat dry. Cut into slices about ¾ inch thick. In a small bowl, combine onion, 3 cloves garlic, ½ cup olive oil, 3 tablespoons lemon juice and thyme; stir well. Add salt and pepper to taste. Brush marinade over the lamb slices, place meat in a bowl and cover with foil. Refrigerate overnight. Remove meat from marinade; lightly brush off onion mixture. Heat vegetable oil in a skillet; brown lamb in batches, 2 to 3 minutes on each side. Place in a bowl and sprinkle with pepper. Return skillet to heat. Add marinade, water and wine. Stir until heated through. Season with sugar and pour marinade over lamb; let cool. Baste meat from time to time with the marinade. Dice tomatoes and place in a large bowl; add the remaining 2 to 3 crushed garlic cloves. In a small bowl, whisk remaining olive oil and lemon juice. Season to taste with salt, pepper and tarragon. Pour over tomatoes and marinate for 20 to 30 minutes. Pour off excess liquid. Remove lamb from marinade. Arrange on a large, deep platter. Pour a little of the marinade over the meat. Surround with tomatoes. In a small serving bowl, combine sour cream, whipping cream and yogurt; mix well. Season to taste with salt and pepper. Serve separately. Serve with pita bread.

Helpful Hints

Run out of long matches to light deep candles? Light an uncooked piece of spaghetti to get into hard-to-reach places.

Cold Stuffed Pork Roast

Makes 8 to 10 servings

1 cup finely chopped onion
1 clove garlic, minced
3 strips bacon, finely chopped
   Olive *or* vegetable oil
1½ to 2 cups seedless grapes
1 cup chopped fresh mush-
   rooms
1 cup soft bread crumbs
1 large egg, lightly beaten
¼ cup minced fresh parsley
½ teaspoon crumbled dried
   thyme
½ teaspoon crumbled dried
   rosemary
   Salt and freshly ground
   black pepper to taste
1 2½ to 3-pound boneless
   pork roast
   Grape clusters

Preheat oven to 375° F. Sauté onion, garlic and bacon in 1 tablespoon olive oil until onion is tender and bacon is crisp. Stir in grapes, mushrooms, bread crumbs, egg, parsley, thyme, rosemary, salt and pepper to taste; set aside. Place pork roast fat side down; slice pork horizontally, being careful not to cut all the way through. Open pork to lie flat and spread with grape mixture. Roll up lengthwise; tie with string every 2 inches. Brush with more olive oil; sprinkle with additional thyme and rosemary. Place on rack in roasting pan. Roast, uncovered, for 1½ hours or until meat thermometer registers 170°. Cool. Cover and refrigerate. Slice to serve; garnish with grape clusters.

Caraway Pork Roast

Makes about 4 servings

2 pounds pork shoulder roast
   Salt
   Pepper
1 teaspoon caraway seed
1 large onion, peeled and
   diced
1 celery rib, diced
2 tablespoons Kümmel brandy

Preheat oven to 400° F. Rinse meat and pat dry. Rub with salt and pepper to taste; rub in caraway seed. Place meat on a large piece of heavy-duty foil; top with onion and celery. Wrap meat loosely; seal foil tightly. Roast for about 1¾ hours. Remove from oven. Let rest in foil for about 10 minutes. Open foil to let meat cool. Pour off cooking juices, strain and let cool. Degrease juices and combine with brandy. Correct seasoning with salt and pepper. Slice meat; arrange on a serving platter. Spoon cooking juices over meat. Serve with a salad, rye rolls and butter.

Fillet of Beef with Herbs

Makes 4 servings

2 pounds trimmed center-cut beef tenderloin
2 onions, peeled and minced
1 clove garlic, peeled and minced
¼ cup prepared mustard
1 teaspoon crushed green peppercorns
Salt
3 to 4 tablespoons chopped parsley, chives, and sage

Preheat oven to 425° F. Rinse tenderloin; pat dry. Place in a buttered ovenproof dish. In a small bowl, combine onion, garlic, mustard and peppercorns. Add salt to taste. Stir in chopped herbs; spread over meat. Roast for 25 to 30 minutes. Remove from oven; let cool. Slice meat and arrange on a platter.

Herbed Beef Roast

Makes 8 to 10 servings

4 pounds prime rump roast
Salt
Pepper
2 cloves garlic, peeled and crushed
2 tablespoons prepared mustard
Marjoram
Thyme
Basil
Sage

Preheat oven to 325° F. Rinse meat; pat dry. Rub with salt and pepper to taste. In a small bowl, mix garlic with mustard; spread over meat. Sprinkle with herbs to taste. Place meat in a roasting pan, fat side up. Insert meat thermometer in center. Roast, uncovered, for 1½ to 2 hours or until thermometer registers 150° for medium rare or 160° for medium. Remove from oven; let cool.

Ham Baked in Foil

Makes 8 to 10 servings

1 6-pound fully cooked ham, skinned
15 cloves
2 to 3 cloves garlic, peeled and chopped
1 to 2 bay leaves, crumbled

Preheat oven to between 375° and 400° F. Trim excess fat. Score ham in a diamond pattern. Stud with cloves and sprinkle with garlic and bay leaves. Loosely wrap in heavy-duty foil; seal tightly. Bake for about 2 hours. Remove from oven. Let rest for about 10 minutes; open foil. Serve hot or cold.

Fresh Ham Roast

Makes 8 to 10 servings

4 pounds fresh ham, boned
2 to 3 cloves garlic, peeled and crushed
¼ cup Dijon-style mustard
¼ cup chopped parsley
    Pepper
    Basil
    Thyme
    Marjoram
    Ground rosemary

Rinse meat; pat dry. In a small bowl, combine garlic, mustard and parsley. Add remaining ingredients to taste. Spread over roast. Let stand at room temperature for about 1 hour. Preheat oven to between 375° and 400° F. Insert meat thermometer in thickest part of roast. Wrap meat loosely in heavy-duty foil; seal tightly. Roast for 2½ hours or until thermometer registers 170° F. Remove from oven. Let rest for 10 minutes; open foil. Let cool or serve hot.

Meat Loaf with Green Peppercorns

Makes 5 to 6 servings

1 hard roll
1 medium onion, peeled and diced
4 slices bacon, diced
¾ pound ground beef
½ pound ground pork
3 eggs
1 teaspoon dried marjoram
1 teaspoon dried thyme
1 tablespoon crushed green peppercorns
1 teaspoon salt, *or* to taste
    Pepper
1 cup cooked carrots, diced
8 sprigs parsley, minced *or* finely chopped
1 tablespoon green peppercorns, optional

Soak roll in cold water; squeeze and tear into small pieces. In a large bowl, mix with onion, bacon, ground meats, eggs, herbs and peppercorns. Add salt and pepper to taste. Preheat oven to 350° F. Spread half the meat mixture in a 9 x 5-inch loaf pan. Arrange carrots over meat and sprinkle with parsley. Top with remaining meat. With the handle of a cooking spoon, make an indentation the length of the meat loaf and fill with whole green peppercorns. Bake for 1 to 1¼ hours. Drain accumulated liquid. Unmold. Serve sliced.

Breaded Pork Chops
Makes 4 servings

4 pork chops, about 6 ounces
  each
Salt
Pepper
1 to 2 tablespoons flour
1 egg, lightly beaten
⅓ cup finely ground bread
  crumbs
3 tablespoons shortening

Rinse chops; pat dry. Pound meat lightly. Season to taste with salt and pepper. Dredge in flour, dip in egg, and coat with bread crumbs. Heat shortening in a skillet large enough to hold the chops. Fry chops for 7 to 8 minutes on each side. Turn over several times during frying. Serve hot or cold.

Pork Chops Stuffed with Pineapple
Makes 4 servings

4 thick pork loin chops
4 canned pineapple slices,
  drained
4 slices smoked ham
Salt
Pepper
1 tablespoon vegetable oil
1 tablespoon margarine
Parsley

Rinse pork chops and pat dry. Cut a pocket in each chop from the fat side. Wrap pineapple slices in ham; stuff into pockets and secure openings with toothpicks. Season chops to taste with salt and pepper. Heat oil and margarine in a skillet; add chops and brown on each side for 7 or 8 minutes or until cooked through. Arrange chops on a platter; garnish with parsley. Serve hot or cold.

Roast Beef Tenderloin
Makes 6 servings

½ cup oil
½ cup Burgundy wine
2 tablespoons grated onion
1 clove garlic, minced
1½ teaspoons salt
5 drops Tabasco, optional
1 4 to 4½-pound beef
  tenderloin

Combine all ingredients and allow beef to marinate in refrigerator at least 2 hours. Remove from sauce. Preheat oven to 450° F. Place meat in a shallow pan and brush with marinade. Bake for 15 minutes. Reduce temperature to 350°. Baste with marinade occasionally and continue baking for 35 minutes for medium rare, or less time for rare. Serve at room temperature.

Roast Beef with Horseradish Sauce

Makes 8 servings

1 3½ to 4-pound boneless round rump roast
¼ teaspoon crumbled dried basil
¼ teaspoon crumbled dried marjoram
Salt and pepper
4 carrots, cut into ¼-inch thick slices
4 potatoes, sliced
1 small onion, separated into rings
Horseradish Sauce
(recipe below)

Preheat oven to 325° F. Rub roast with basil, marjoram, salt and pepper to taste. Place on a rack in a shallow roasting pan; cover with foil. Pour 1 cup water in bottom of roasting pan. Place roast in oven and bake for 1½ hours. While roast is cooking, place vegetables in a medium saucepan. Cover with water; salt to taste. Bring to a boil; cook for 15 to 20 minutes. Drain vegetables. Place vegetables around roast and baste with accumulated juices. Cook 45 to 50 minutes longer. Prepare Horseradish Sauce. Remove roast and vegetables from oven; set aside to cool. Serve roast and vegetables with Horseradish Sauce.

Horseradish Sauce

Makes 1½ cups sauce

1 cup whipping cream, beaten until stiff
6 tablespoons lemon juice
½ teaspoon salt
¼ teaspoon white pepper
2 tablespoons finely minced onion
4 tablespoons finely grated horseradish
⅓ cup mayonnaise

Place whipping cream in a serving bowl. Add remaining ingredients, one at a time, beating continuously until well mixed. Set aside for 30 minutes before serving. If you prefer, this may be chilled.

Helpful Hints

Fresh mushrooms have closed caps. The gills should not show around the stem.

To treat a red-wine stain, cover immediately with salt or baking soda. Allow to dry, then vacuum.

Roast Beef with Horseradish Sauce, this page

HOW TO CARVE MEATS

Beef Standing Rib Roast

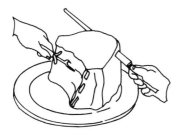  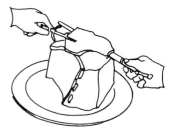

1. Insert fork below top rib. Carve across the "face" of roast to rib bone.

2. With fork still inserted, cut along rib bone with knife to release slice.

3. Slide knife back under slice and, steadying it with fork, lift to side of platter.

Beef Blade Pot Roast

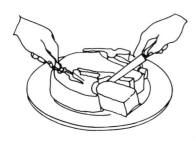  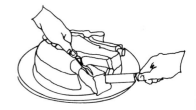

1. Cut between muscles and around bones to remove one solid section of pot roast.

2. Turn section so meat fibers are parallel to platter in order to carve across grain of meat.

3. Holding meat with fork, carve removed section into slices about ¼ inch thick. Repeat.

Shank Half of Ham

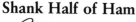 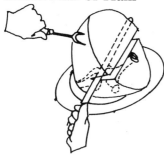 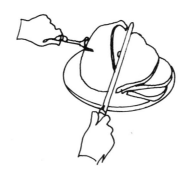 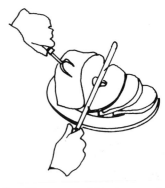

1. With shank at carver's left, turn ham so thick cushion side is up. Cut along top of leg and shank bones and under fork to lift off boneless cushion.

2. Place cushion meat on carving board and make perpendicular slices as illustrated.

3. Cut around leg bone with tip of knife to remove meat from this bone. Turn meat so that thickest side is down. Slice in same manner as cushion piece.

HOW TO CARVE MEATS

Beef Porterhouse Steak

1. Hold steak steady with fork. Use tip of knife to cut closely around bone. Lift bone to one side of platter.

2. Carve across full width of steak, cutting through both top loin and tenderloin. Diagonal slicing (instead of perpendicular) is recommended for thick steaks.

Pork Loin Roast

1. Before roast is brought to table, remove back bone leaving as little meat on it as possible. Place roast on platter with rib side facing so carver can see angle of ribs and make slices accordingly.

2. Insert fork in top of roast. Make slices by cutting closely along each side of rib bone. One slice will contain the rib; the next will be boneless.

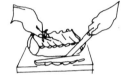

Whole Ham

1. Ham is placed on platter with decorated or fat side up and shank to carver's right. Location of bones in right and left hams may be confusing so double-check location of knee cap, which may be on near or far side of ham. Remove two or three lengthwise slices from thin side of ham which contains knee cap.

2. Turn ham so that it rests on surface just cut. Make perpendicular slices down to leg bone or lift off boneless cushion as in method illustrated for Picnic Shoulder.

3. Release slices by cutting along leg bone.

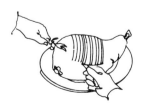

Picnic Shoulder

Carving is the same for both a roasted (baked) smoked picnic and a roasted (baked) fresh picnic.

1. Remove a lengthwise slice as shown here. Turn picnic so that it rests on surface just cut. Cut down to arm bone at a point near elbow bone. Turn knife and cut along arm bone to remove boneless arm meat.

2. Carve boneless arm meat by making perpendicular slices from top of meat down to cutting board.

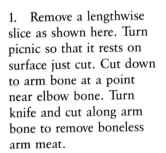

3. Remove the meat from each side of the arm bone. Then carve the two boneless pieces.

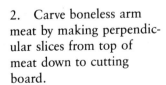

Beefsteak Tartare

Makes 6 to 8 servings

1 to 1½ pounds freshly
  ground beef tenderloin
1 tablespoon vegetable oil
1 to 2 teaspoons prepared
  mustard
1 teaspoon crushed green
  peppercorns
  Salt
  Vinegar
  Paprika
6 to 8 egg yolks
  Onion rings
  Capers
  Dill pickles
  Chives, chopped
  Anchovy fillets
  Freshly ground pepper
  Paprika
  Parsley

In a large bowl, combine ground meat with oil, mustard and green peppercorns. Season to taste with salt, vinegar and paprika. Divide into portions and arrange on a platter or on individual serving plates. Make an indentation in the center of each portion and fill with 1 egg yolk. Serve accompaniments in separate glass bowls. Use parsley for garnish.

Beef Rolls

Makes 2 to 4 servings

4 lean bottom round slices,
  about 5 ounces each
  Dijon-style mustard
4 Chinese cabbage leaves the
  size of the meat, blanched
8 slices bacon
2 onions, peeled and chopped
2 teaspoons green pepper-
  corns, crushed
2 tablespoons chopped mixed
  herbs
3 tablespoons vegetable oil
½ cup red wine

Spread meat thinly with mustard. Cover with cabbage leaves. Top each with 2 slices bacon. Mix onion, pepper and herbs; distribute over bacon. Roll up slices; tie with string. Heat oil in the pressure cooker. Brown rolls on all sides. Add wine, close lid and cook meat for about 15 minutes. Let cool in pan juices. Remove string. Slice rolls thickly. Arrange, overlapping, on a platter. Degrease pan juices; spoon juice over meat. Goes well with French bread and salad.

Beefsteak Tartare, this page

Game and Poultry

Saddle of Venison with Orange Sauce

(Illustrated previous page)
Makes about 6 servings

1 3-pound saddle of venison
Salt
2½ tablespoons soft butter *or* margarine
3 ounces sliced bacon *or* salt pork, blanched
2 juniper berries, crushed
1 onion, peeled and quartered
Hot water
Liver paté, optional
⅔ cup white wine, divided
1 stick cinnamon
Sugar
1 envelope unflavored gelatin
1 11-ounce can mandarin oranges, drained
12 canned pear halves, drained
1 cup orange juice
1 tablespoon cornstarch
1 10-ounce jar lingonberries, divided
Grated orange rind
Prepared mustard
Salt
Pepper
Lemon juice
Parsley

Preheat oven to between 425° and 450° F. Rinse meat and pat dry; remove skin. Rub venison with salt; brush with butter. Rinse roasting pan with water; distribute half the bacon slices over the pan. Add meat; cover with remaining bacon. Place in oven. When pan juices start to brown, add juniper berries and onion to pan. When heated through, add a little hot water. Baste roast with pan juices from time to time; add more water as needed. Roast venison for 35 to 50 minutes. Remove from oven. Let rest for about 10 minutes. Remove warm meat from bone in one piece; let cool. Slice meat and reassemble saddle. May be spread with liver paté. In a small saucepan, simmer ½ cup wine with the cinnamon and sugar to taste; let cool. Sprinkle gelatin over remaining wine. Let stand for 10 minutes. Heat in a small pan, stirring, until dissolved. Add gelatin to cinnamon and wine; chill until liquid starts to thicken. Place roast on a cake rack over a baking sheet or waxed paper; garnish with mandarin oranges placed on top and between slices. Brush with gelatin mixture; spread remaining mixture over cut side of pear halves. Chill. In a small saucepan, gradually stir orange juice into cornstarch. Bring to a boil, stirring; cook for about 1 minute. Let cool. Force 2 to 3 tablespoons of the lingonberries through a sieve; add to orange sauce. Season to taste with all remaining ingredients except parsley. Place roast on a large platter. Fill pear halves with lingonberries; add to platter. Garnish with parsley. Serve sauce separately.

Glazed Chicken

Makes about 4 servings

1 3-pound roasting chicken
Salt
Pepper
1 tablespoon butter *or* margarine, melted
1 tablespoon paprika
½ cup water
Pineapple, fresh *or* canned
Cherries, fresh *or* canned
1 envelope unflavored gelatin
3 tablespoons cold water

Preheat oven to 400° F. Rinse chicken; pat dry. Cut in half and season to taste with salt and pepper inside and out. Combine melted butter with paprika and brush on chicken. Place chicken halves in a roasting pan skin side up. Roast for about 35 minutes or until chicken tests done; baste occasionally with pan juices. If needed, add a little water to pan. Set aside to cool. Add ½ cup water to pan; deglaze. Pour into a small bowl and let cool; degrease. Divide chicken into 6 portions. Remove bones, if desired. Arrange on a serving platter and garnish with pineapple pieces and cherries. In a small bowl sprinkle gelatin over cold water. Place into a larger container with hot water until dissolved. Heat pan juices to almost boiling; stir in gelatin. Chill until mixture starts to thicken; brush over chicken pieces.

Breaded Turkey Cutlets

Makes 4 servings

4 turkey cutlets, about 5 ounces each
Salt
White pepper
Curry powder
¼ to ⅓ cup flour
1 egg, lightly beaten
⅓ cup finely ground bread crumbs
⅓ cup clarified butter
Lettuce leaves, washed and dried
Pineapple slices, halved
Mint leaves

Rinse meat; pat dry. Season to taste with salt, pepper and curry powder. Dredge in flour, dip in egg and coat with bread crumbs. Press crumbs firmly into meat. Heat butter in a skillet; fry cutlets for 6 minutes on each side until golden brown. Drain on paper towels; let cool. Arrange lettuce leaves on a serving platter. Place cutlets and pineapple slices on top. Garnish with mint leaves.

Fried Chicken with Potato Salad

Makes about 4 servings

1½ pounds potatoes, boiled,
   still hot
1 cup water
2 teaspoons salt
2 tablespoons herbed vinegar
   Pinch of pepper
1 teaspoon sugar
   Generous ¼ cup mayonnaise
1 medium apple
2 medium dill pickles, sliced
1 onion, peeled and minced
   Salt
   Pepper
   Vinegar
   Tomato wedges
   Parsley
1 2-pound chicken, cut into
   serving pieces
1 egg
   Pinch of pepper
   Pinch of paprika
1 teaspoon salt
   Finely ground bread crumbs
   Vegetable oil

Peel and slice potatoes while still warm. Bring water to a boil in a small saucepan, add next four ingredients and stir until dissolved. Pour dressing over potatoes; marinate for 15 minutes. Remove potatoes with a slotted spoon. In a small bowl, blend remaining marinade with mayonnaise. Peel, quarter and core apple; slice thinly crosswise. Add to potatoes along with pickles and onion. Fold in mayonnaise. Correct seasoning with salt, pepper and vinegar. Garnish with tomato wedges and parsley. Rinse chicken pieces; pat dry. In a medium-size bowl, beat egg lightly with pepper, paprika and salt. Dip chicken in egg; coat with bread crumbs. In an electric skillet, heat about 2 inches of oil to 375° F. Fry chicken submerged, in batches, for about 15 minutes. Test for doneness. Drain on paper towels. Let cool, or serve hot.

Turkey Salad

Makes 6 to 8 servings

2 pounds cooked turkey meat
1 kosher dill pickle, diced
¼ cup minced green onion
1¼ pounds boiled potatoes,
   diced
½ cup sour cream
½ cup mayonnaise
2½ teaspoons dried dill
1 tomato, cut into wedges
1 hard-boiled egg, cut into
   wedges
6 black olives

Combine turkey, pickle, onion and potatoes with sour cream and mayonnaise. Add 2 teaspoons dill and mix well. Mound on platter or shallow serving bowl. Garnish with tomato, egg and black olives. Sprinkle with remaining dill.

Stuffed Goose Breast

Makes about 4 servings

1 whole boneless goose breast,
about 1½ pounds
Salt
Pepper
1 teaspoon hot mustard
1 to 2 tablespoons butter
1 onion, peeled and chopped
¼ pound calf's liver, chopped
2 tablespoons brandy
1 tablespoon chopped
pistachios
1 skinless pre-cooked
bratwurst sausage
2 to 3 tablespoons whipping
cream
Hot water
Cold salted water
Orange sections
Parsley

Rinse meat; pat dry. Rub cut side with salt and pepper to taste; spread with mustard. In a skillet, heat butter and sauté onion and liver for about 2 minutes. Add brandy; remove from heat and let cool. Add pistachios. Preheat oven to 400° F. Chop bratwurst; place in blender jar with cream. Process on high until smooth; stir into liver mixture. Place filling on one half of the breast, fold the other half over; close with toothpicks. Place meat on a rack in a roasting pan rinsed with water. Place in center of preheated oven. When pan juices begin to brown, add a little hot water. Baste meat with the pan juices from time to time. Add more water as needed. Total roasting time is 2 to 2½ hours, depending on age of bird. About 10 minutes before meat is done brush skin with cold salted water; turn heat up to crisp skin. Let meat cool. Remove toothpicks; slice meat thinly. Arrange on a platter and garnish with orange sections and parsley.

Stuffed Cornish Hens

Makes 2 to 4 servings

2 Rock Cornish hens, thawed
3 small French rolls
2 eggs
Grated rind of ½ lemon
Salt
Pepper
Pinch of thyme
1 tablespoon chopped parsley
1½ tablespoons unsalted butter,
melted
½ tablespoon lemon juice
¼ teaspoon salt

Preheat oven to 375° F. Rinse hens; pat dry. Soak rolls in cold water; squeeze. Tear rolls apart; combine with eggs and lemon rind. Season to taste with salt and pepper; add thyme and parsley. Stuff hens; close cavities with skewers. Mix butter with lemon juice and salt. Add pepper to taste. Place hens on rack in roasting pan; brush with some of the butter. Roast for 1 hour. Brush with remaining butter once or twice during roasting. Remove from oven. Chill.

Chicken Breasts in Lime Sauce

Makes 4 servings

4 chicken breast halves,
  skinned and boned
Salt
White pepper
Flour
1 egg, lightly beaten
4 ounces chopped blanched
  almonds
2½ tablespoons clarified butter
  or margarine
⅔ cup sour cream
⅔ cup whipping cream, lightly
  beaten
1 tablespoon mint leaves,
  chopped
1 tablespoon lemon juice
2 tablespoons dry vermouth
  Grated rind of ½ lime
4 tablespoons freshly squeezed
  lime juice
Sugar
Boston lettuce leaves,
  washed and dried
2 tablespoons green peppercorns
Mint leaves
Lime slices

Wash chicken breasts; pat dry. Season to taste with salt and pepper. Dredge in flour, dip in egg and coat with almonds. In a skillet, heat butter and brown meat for about 4 minutes on each side; let cool. In a small bowl, combine sour cream, cream, mint, lemon juice and vermouth; stir in grated rind and lime juice. Season to taste with salt and sugar. Arrange chicken breasts on lettuce leaves; top with half the lime sauce. Sprinkle with green peppercorns and garnish with mint leaves and lime slices. Serve remaining sauce separately.

Rolled Turkey Roast

Makes about 6 servings

1 frozen rolled turkey roast,
  thawed
1 tablespoon vegetable oil
Salt
Pepper
Paprika
Semi-hot mustard, optional

Place roast on spit or in grill basket. In a small bowl, combine oil, salt, pepper and paprika to taste. Add mustard; brush over meat. Depending on thickness of roast, grill 45 to 60 minutes on electric grill, about 50 minutes on gas grill. Baste with drippings from time to time. Let cool.

Chicken Breasts in Lime Sauce, this page

Turkey Leg with Chive Dressing
Makes 3 to 4 servings

1 or 2 turkey legs, about 2 pounds
1½ quarts water
1 bunch parsley
6 peppercorns
5 to 6 carrots, scraped and quartered lengthwise
2 to 3 celery ribs, trimmed, strings removed
2 leeks, root ends trimmed
1 small cauliflower, trimmed, florets separated
2 hard-boiled eggs, peeled and riced
2 teaspoons semi-hot mustard
½ cup vegetable oil
Vinegar
Salt
Pepper
½ cup chopped chives
Parsley for garnish

Rinse meat; pat dry. In a large saucepan, bring water to a boil. Add turkey, parsley and peppercorns. Return to boil; simmer for 50 minutes. Cut carrot sticks into 1½-inch pieces; cut celery into 2-inch pieces. Add vegetables to pot, return to boil; simmer for 10 minutes. Halve leeks lengthwise; remove greens to within 3 inches of stalk. Wash stalks carefully and cut into 2-inch lengths. Add leeks to pot together with cauliflower florets. Return to boil; simmer for 15 minutes more. Remove from heat; let cool in liquid. In a small bowl, combine riced eggs with mustard; gradually add oil. Dressing should thicken. Season to taste with vinegar, salt and pepper; add chives. Drain turkey and vegetables well. Arrange vegetables on a platter; top with dressing. Slice turkey meat and arrange over vegetables. Garnish with parsley. May be served with French bread.

Sesame Seed Chicken Wings
Makes 6 to 12 servings

2 eggs
¾ cup flour
½ teaspoon salt
¾ cup cold water
4 cups peanut or corn oil
12 to 16 chicken wings
½ cup sesame seed
Bottled sweet-sour sauce, optional

Beat eggs; gradually add flour and salt. Add water slowly, and beat until smooth and thin. Refrigerate for 30 minutes before using. Heat oil to 375° F. in skillet or deep fryer. Dip each chicken wing in batter; sprinkle with sesame seed. Deep fry 4 wings at a time for 10 to 12 minutes, turning several times. Remove from oil and drain on paper towels. Repeat until all pieces are fried. Serve with bottled sweet-sour sauce, if desired.

Saddle of Rabbit Waldorf
Makes 2 to 3 servings

1 saddle of rabbit, about 1¼
  pounds
8 crushed juniper berries
  Salt
  Pepper
1 to 2 tablespoons softened
  butter
  Waldorf Salad (see page 42)
1 Kiwi, sliced
  Cherries

Preheat oven to 400° F. Rinse meat; pat dry. Skin carefully. Partially separate meat from center bone; lightly push outward. Rub with juniper berries and season to taste with salt and pepper. Brush with softened butter. Place in a roasting pan rinsed with water; roast for 10 minutes. Turn off heat. Remove saddle from oven and wrap in heavy-duty foil. Return to oven to cool. Meat will stay juicy and rosy in the center. Remove meat from bones and slice thinly. Use a large serving platter; arrange Waldorf Salad around outside; place sliced meat in center. Garnish with Kiwi and cherries.
Tip: When preparing saddle in advance, it is best to glaze it with Wine Aspic (see page 68).

Chicken with Pistachio Stuffing
Makes 4 servings

1 3-pound chicken
2 slices white bread, diced
3 tablespoons port
⅓ pound chicken livers,
  trimmed
3 ounces pistachios, ground
¼ pound ground beef
2 small eggs
  Salt
  Pepper
2 tablespoons vegetable oil
½ teaspoon paprika
  Pinch of curry powder
½ cup chicken broth (instant)
  Pistachios

Preheat oven to 400° F. Rinse chicken; pat dry. Sprinkle bread with port. Grind chicken livers; in a mixing bowl, combine with bread, ground pistachios, ground beef and eggs. Season to taste with salt and pepper. Mix well. Stuff chicken; close cavity. In a small bowl, combine oil with paprika and curry powder; brush over chicken. Place in oven on a roasting pan rinsed with water. When pan juices start to brown, add a little hot broth. Baste chicken occasionally. Add more broth as needed. Roast for about 50 minutes; check for doneness. Remove skewers. Cut chicken into serving pieces and arrange on a serving platter. Garnish with pistachios.

French Turkey Roll-ups

Makes about 4 servings

16 thin turkey medallions
Oregano
Thyme
White pepper
8 bacon slices, halved
3 tablespoons olive oil
Salt
8 ounces eggplant
2 to 3 onions, peeled and diced
1 large *or* 2 small red bell peppers, halved, seeded and diced
2 medium tomatoes, peeled, quartered, seeded and diced
1 clove garlic, peeled and crushed
Basil
Lemon wedges
Lemon juice, optional

Rinse meat; pat dry. Season to taste with next 3 ingredients. Top medallions with halved bacon slices, roll up and tie with string. Heat oil in a skillet; brown meat on all sides for about 5 minutes. Season to taste with salt. Remove string; let meat cool. Leave pan juices in skillet. Dice eggplant and sprinkle with salt. Set aside for 10 minutes; pat dry. Reheat pan juices. Add onion and cook until limp. Add eggplant and bell pepper; sauté for 10 to 15 minutes. Add a little water if needed. Add tomatoes and garlic; season with basil to taste. Cook for 10 minutes more. Correct seasoning with salt and pepper; cool. To serve, place vegetables in a shallow bowl and arrange turkey rolls on top. Garnish with lemon wedges; sprinkle meat with lemon juice.

Chicken-Stuffed Avocados

Makes 4 servings

2 avocados
2 cups diced cooked chicken
1 cup diced celery
¾ cup mayonnaise
1 teaspoon lemon juice
¼ teaspoon salt
⅛ teaspoon pepper
¼ cup sweet relish
Lettuce leaves
Shredded lettuce
Hard-boiled eggs, sliced
Olives
Tomatoes, sliced

Cut avocados in half lengthwise. Peel and place in salt water for a few minutes, or dip in lemon juice so that avocado does not turn dark. Mix chicken, celery, mayonnaise, lemon juice, salt, pepper, and relish together. Fill avocados with mixture. Place atop lettuce leaves on a platter with shredded lettuce and garnish with hard-boiled egg slices, olives, and tomato.

*French Turkey Roll-ups,
this page*

Turkey Quiche
Makes 6 servings

1 cup chopped, cooked turkey
2 tablespoons chopped green
   onion
1 3-ounce package cream
   cheese, softened
2 tablespoons dry vermouth
1 9-inch pie crust, unbaked
4 eggs
1 cup heavy cream
½ cup milk
½ teaspoon salt
¼ teaspoon crushed rosemary

Combine turkey with onion, cream cheese, and vermouth in a mixing bowl; spread in crust. Beat eggs in a small bowl with cream; add milk and seasonings, and pour over turkey mixture. Bake at 450° F. for 10 minutes. Reduce temperature to 350° and bake for 40 more minutes. Cool.

Curried Chicken or Turkey
Makes 6 to 8 servings

2 cups minced cooked chicken
   or turkey
½ to ¾ cup mayonnaise
¼ cup minced celery
1 to 2 teaspoons curry powder
6 to 8 croissants

Combine first 4 ingredients in large mixing bowl. Chill. Serve in croissants.

Roast Turkey Drumsticks
Makes 2 to 4 servings

2 to 4 turkey drumsticks
   Butter
   Salt and paprika to taste
3 stalks celery
1 onion, thinly sliced
2 cups chicken stock *or*
   bouillon
1 16-ounce can tomato sauce

Rinse drumsticks in cold water. Rub with butter and season with salt and paprika. Place in a greased baking dish. Cut celery in julienne slices and arrange with onion around drumsticks. Add chicken bouillon and tomato sauce. Cover. Bake in a 350° F. oven for 1½ to 2 hours. Check to see that drumsticks are moist and replace liquid with water as drumsticks cook. When meat is tender, remove drumsticks and cool.

Tropical Chicken
Makes 4 servings

3 tablespoons butter
4 tablespoons flour
1 cup chicken broth
1 cup milk
½ teaspoon salt
½ teaspoon paprika
⅛ teaspoon pepper
1½ cups diced cooked Sherried
    Chicken (recipe below)
½ cup diced pineapple
6 Pineapple Boats (recipe
    below)
½ cup slivered almonds
    Grated Parmesan cheese

Melt butter in top of double boiler. Add flour all at once and stir over low heat until blended. Add cold broth and milk all at once and simmer, stirring constantly, until thickened. Add seasonings and Sherried Chicken; heat thoroughly. Add more salt and pepper if desired. Remove from heat; blend in diced pineapple. Fill the Pineapple Boats with the poultry mixture, dividing evenly. Top with slivered almonds and sprinkle lightly with cheese. Place on a large serving platter. Prepare the day of serving, as the sauce separates when refrigerated.

Sherried Chicken

2 whole chicken breasts,
    boned, skinned and halved
    Seasoned salt as desired
3 tablespoons butter
⅓ cup sherry
1 4-ounce can button mush-
    rooms

Lightly sprinkle chicken with seasoned salt. Brown butter in a saucepan and add sherry and liquid from mushrooms. Pour the heated sauce over the chicken (add the mushrooms if you wish). Cover and bake at 350° F. for 1 hour.

Pineapple Boats

3 whole fresh pineapples

Cut pineapples in half lengthwise, leaving leafy tops attached. Separate the leaves gently with your fingers and use a firm sawing motion to cut. When split, use a grapefruit knife (curved, saw-toothed blade) to hollow out fruit from shell. Reserve fruit, but cut away and discard the tough central core and any dark "eyes."

Fruit-Glazed Chicken Legs

Makes 4 servings

4 chicken legs, about ½ pound each
2 tablespoons vegetable oil
½ teaspoon paprika
Pinch of curry powder
Salt to taste
Pepper to taste
½ cup hot water
1 small can mandarin oranges, drained
1 small can sliced peaches, drained, syrup reserved
1 small can pineapple slices, halved
Maraschino cherries
1 envelope unflavored gelatin
3 tablespoons white wine
Lemon balm *or* mint leaves

Preheat oven to 400° F. Rinse chicken; pat dry. In a small bowl, combine oil with paprika, curry powder, salt and pepper. Brush mixture over legs. Put on rack in a roasting pan rinsed with water. Place in center of oven. When pan juices start browning, add a little hot water. Baste chicken occasionally. Add more water as needed. Roast for 25 to 30 minutes or until done. Remove from oven; let cool. Place chicken legs on a cake rack set on waxed paper; garnish with fruit. In a saucepan, add enough water to reserved syrup to make a scant cup. Sprinkle gelatin over wine; place in a larger container with hot water until dissolved. Heat syrup and stir in gelatin. Chill until mixture starts to thicken. Brush over chicken and fruit. Repeat until meat and fruit are completely covered with aspic. Let remaining aspic set; dice. Arrange legs on a platter. Garnish with diced aspic and lemon balm or mint leaves.

Baked Chicken Paté

Makes about 6 servings

1 medium onion, chopped
1 clove garlic, minced
2 eggs
1 pound chicken livers
¼ cup flour
½ teaspoon allspice
1 teaspoon salt
½ teaspoon pepper
¼ cup butter
1 cup light cream

Place all ingredients in a blender; blend until smooth. Pour into a greased 1-quart baking dish; cover. Set in pan of hot water and bake in a 325° F. oven for 3 hours. Cool, then chill. Unmold and serve with unsalted crackers or Melba toast.

Fruit-Glazed Chicken Legs, this page

Chicken Potato Salad

Makes 6 servings

4 cups boiled potatoes, diced
2 cups chicken, diced
1½ cups celery, diced
1 tablespoon lemon juice
½ teaspoon salt
¼ teaspoon pepper
1 tablespoon Worcestershire
   sauce
1½ cups mayonnaise
½ cup pickle relish
   Lettuce leaves
   Shredded lettuce
   Hard-boiled eggs, sliced
   Olives
   Tomatoes, cut in wedges

Mix first 9 ingredients together and chill well. Place on lettuce leaves and surround with shredded lettuce. Garnish with hard-boiled egg slices, olives, and tomato wedges, if desired.

Chicken and Macaroni Salad

Makes 6 servings

1 7-ounce package ring
   macaroni
1 cup cubed cooked chicken
1 cup diced celery
2 teaspoons chopped parsley
1¼ cups mayonnaise
1 tablespoon sugar
1 cup diced apple *or* pineapple
½ cup chopped nuts, optional
1 teaspoon salt
½ cup pickle relish, drained
   Lettuce leaves
   Hard-boiled eggs, sliced
   Green olives

Cook macaroni until just tender. Rinse with cold water; drain. Gently mix with next 9 ingredients and place on lettuce. Garnish with hard-boiled egg slices and olives.

HOW TO CARVE POULTRY

Standard Style

1. To remove leg (drumstick and thigh), hold the drumstick firmly with fingers, pulling gently away from body of bird. At the same time cut through skin between leg and body.

2. Press leg away from body with flat side of knife. Then cut through joint joining leg to backbone and skin on the back. Hold leg on service plate with drumstick at a convenient angle to plate. Separate drumstick and thigh by cutting down through the joint to the plate.

3. Slice drumstick meat. Hold drumstick upright at a convenient angle to plate and cut down, turning drumstick to get uniform slices. Drumsticks and thighs from smaller birds are usually served whole.

4. Slice thigh meat. Hold thigh firmly on plate with a fork. Cut slices of meat parallel to the bone.

5. Cut into white meat parallel to wing. Make a cut deep into the breast to the body frame parallel to and close to the wing.

6. Slice white meat. Beginning at front, starting halfway up the breast, cut thin slices of white meat down to the cut made parallel to the wing. The slices will fall away from the bird as they are cut to this line.

Side Style

1. Remove wing tip and first joint. Grasp wing tip firmly with fingers, lift up, and cut between first and second joint. Place wing tip and first joint portion on side of platter. Leave second joint attached to bird.

2. Remove the drumstick. Grasp end of drumstick and lift it up and away from the body, disjointing it from the thigh. Thigh is left attached to the bird. Place drumstick on service plate for slicing. Hold drumstick upright at an angle and cut down toward plate, parallel with bone, turning to make even slices.

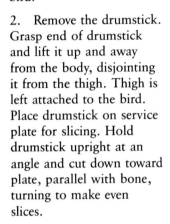

3. Anchoring the fork where it is most convenient to steady the bird, cut slices of thigh meat parallel to the body until the bone is reached. Run the point of the knife around the thigh bone, lift up with fork, and remove bone.

4. Begin at front end of bird and slice white meat until the wing socket is exposed. Remove second joint of wing. Continue slicing until enough slices have been provided, or until the breastbone is reached.

5. Remove stuffing from hole cut into cavity under thigh. Slit the thin tissue in the thigh region with tip of knife and make an opening large enough for a serving spoon.

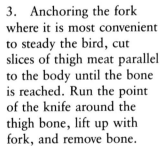

Courtesy Poultry & Egg National Board

Sauces, Dressings, Dips, and Flavored Butters

Sauces, Dressings, Dips, and Flavored Butters

Sauces, dressings, dips, and flavored butters add a dash of elegance when entertaining with buffets and smorgasbords. Sauces and dressings can spice up salads and also make great side dishes for dipping. The flavored butters are delicious whether spread on sandwiches or served on the side with a variety of meat and fish dishes. The butters can also be used in the preparation to baste meats and fish while cooking. This chapter provides recipes for many of these accompaniments as well as serving suggestions for the foods they will most enhance.

Herb Dip

(Illustrated previous page)
Makes about ⅔ cup dip

3 anchovy fillets
1 tablespoon capers
10 stuffed olives
3 egg yolks, lightly beaten
1 teaspoon Dijon-style mustard
1 to 2 tablespoons vinegar
Salt
Pepper
¼ cup vegetable oil
4 to 5 teaspoons minced mixed herbs
2 tomatoes, peeled, seeded and diced

Finely chop the first three ingredients. In a small bowl, mix egg yolks, mustard and vinegar; add salt and pepper to taste. Stir in oil by the tablespoonful; cream well. Combine with herbs and first 3 ingredients and fold in tomatoes. Serve with raw vegetables or use as a dressing with baked potatoes.

Aioli Sauce

Makes about ½ cup sauce

½ cup mayonnaise
4 to 5 cloves garlic, peeled and puréed
Salt
Red pepper
Lemon juice

In a small bowl, combine mayonnaise and garlic. Season to taste with salt, pepper and lemon juice. Serve with roast beef, broiled fish or cooked vegetables.

Herbed Yogurt Dressing

Makes about 1½ cups dressing

1⅓ cups yogurt
2 to 3 shallots *or* 1 onion, peeled and minced
1 to 2 cloves garlic, peeled and crushed
2 tablespoons chopped dill
2 tablespoons chopped parsley
2 tablespoons chopped basil *or* ½ tablespoon dried basil
3 tablespoons lemon juice
3 tablespoons olive oil
Salt, pepper and sugar

In a small bowl, mix yogurt with shallots, garlic and herbs. Whisk together lemon juice and oil; add to dressing. Season to taste with salt, pepper and sugar. Serve with salads or grilled meats.

Creamy Roquefort Dressing

Makes about ½ cup dressing

1 ounce Roquefort *or* Gorgonzola
¼ cup sour cream
¼ cup whipping cream
Salt
Pepper
Lemon juice

In a small bowl, mash cheese with a fork and mix with sour cream. Gradually blend in cream; season to taste with salt, pepper and lemon juice. Goes well with salads made with radicchio, spinach or endive.

Bombay Dip

Makes about ¾ cup dip

1 medium apple, peeled
Lemon juice
⅓ cup sour cream
⅓ cup whipping cream
1 teaspoon curry powder
Salt
Pepper

Quarter, core and chop apple; sprinkle with a little lemon juice. In a small bowl, mix sour cream with cream; add curry powder and apple. Season to taste with salt and pepper. Goes well with roast chicken.

Cumberland Sauce

Makes about 1½ cups sauce

1 orange
¼ cup port
1 cup currant jelly
½ to 1 teaspoon prepared
   mustard
   Salt
   Pepper
   Lemon juice

Thinly peel zest of orange and cut into narrow strips. In a small saucepan, boil orange strips in a small amount of water for about five minutes; drain and pat dry. Squeeze half of the orange. Combine juice with boiled zest and port. Blend currant jelly and mustard until smooth; add to orange mixture. Season to taste with salt, pepper and lemon juice. Serve with lamb, game or roast beef.

Creamy Mustard Dressing

Makes about ½ cup dressing

½ cup whipping cream
2 teaspoons prepared mustard
   Salt
   Pepper
1 tablespoon lemon juice

In a small bowl, whip cream for about 1 minute. Add mustard and continue whipping until soft peaks form. Season to taste with salt and pepper; stir in lemon juice. Serve with leafy salads or vegetable and meat salads.

Zesty Vinaigrette Dressing

Makes about ½ cup dressing

4 tablespoons vegetable oil
2 tablespoons red wine vinegar
1 teaspoon prepared mustard
1 small onion, peeled and
   minced
2 hard-boiled eggs, peeled and
   chopped
4 sweet gherkins, chopped
2 tablespoons minced parsley
1 teaspoon chopped capers
   Salt
   Pepper

In a small bowl, whisk together oil, vinegar and mustard. Stir in remaining ingredients and season to taste with salt and pepper.

Cumberland Sauce, this page

Chive Butter

Makes about ½ cup butter

4 ounces unsalted butter,
  softened
6 tablespoons finely chopped
  chives
Salt
White pepper

In a small bowl, cream butter; add chives and season to taste with salt and pepper. Goes well with pork chops or fish.

Curry Dressing

Makes about ⅔ cup dressing

⅔ cup yogurt
1 teaspoon prepared mustard
1 teaspoon curry powder
1 to 1½ teaspoons honey
1 tablespoon lemon juice
  Ground coriander
  Salt
  Pepper

In a small bowl, combine yogurt, mustard, curry powder, honey and lemon juice until well mixed. Season to taste with coriander, salt and pepper. Goes well with salads, grilled or broiled meats, or as a dipping sauce for meat fondue.

Walnut Sauce

Makes about 1 cup sauce

⅔ cup sour cream
⅓ cup whipping cream
½ tablespoon lemon juice
  Juice and grated rind of 1
  small orange
  Salt
  Pepper
2 to 3 tablespoons chopped
  walnuts

In a small bowl, combine sour cream with cream. Add juices and orange rind; season to taste with salt and pepper. Stir in walnuts. Serve with broiled meats.

Chive Butter, this page

Basic Mayonnaise

Makes about ½ cup dressing

1 egg yolk
1½ to 2 teaspoons prepared
   mustard
1 tablespoon vinegar *or* lemon
   juice
   Salt, pepper, sugar
½ cup vegetable oil

In a small bowl, whisk together egg yolk, mustard and vinegar. Add salt, pepper and sugar to taste. Whisk in oil drop by drop until mayonnaise thickens. Continue to whisk, adding remaining oil in a steady stream.

Egg Yolk Butter

Makes about ½ cup butter

4 ounces unsalted butter,
   softened
   Yolks of 4 hard-boiled eggs,
   riced
1 shallot, peeled and minced
1 tablespoon finely chopped
   parsley
   Salt
   White pepper

In a small bowl, cream butter with egg yolks, shallot and parsley. Season to taste with salt and pepper.

Herbed Butter

Makes about ½ cup butter

4 ounces unsalted butter,
   softened
1 teaspoon minced onion
1 garlic clove, peeled and
   puréed
1 teaspoon lemon juice
2 teaspoons minced parsley
1 teaspoon minced tarragon
   Salt
   Worcestershire sauce

In a small bowl, cream butter with onion and garlic. Add lemon juice and herbs; season to taste with salt and Worcestershire sauce. Transfer butter to a piece of parchment paper. Fold paper over one side of butter and shape into a log by pressing a knife against the length of the paper toward the butter. Refrigerate until firm. Serve in slices. Goes well with grilled or broiled meats.

Confetti Dip

Makes about ⅔ cup dip

4 ounces cream cheese,
  softened
5 tablespoons buttermilk
1 small tomato, peeled, seeded
  and chopped
1 anchovy fillet, finely
  chopped
2 green pitted olives, chopped
2 black pitted olives, chopped
1 to 2 teaspoons minced onion
  Salt
  Pepper
  Thyme

In a small bowl, beat cream cheese until smooth; gradually stir in buttermilk. Stir in remaining ingredients and season to taste with salt, pepper and thyme.

Lemon Butter

Makes ½ cup butter

4 ounces unsalted butter,
  softened
Grated rind of 1 to 2 lemons
Salt

In a small bowl, cream butter; add grated lemon rind. Season to taste with a small amount of salt. Goes well with fish or on bread with jam.

Green Sauce

Makes about 1½ cups sauce

1 cup mayonnaise
8 spinach leaves, blanched and
  chopped
1 green onion, minced
1 tablespoon minced parsley
1 tablespoon minced watercress leaves
1 teaspoon minced basil *or* ¼
  teaspoon dried basil
1 teaspoon minced dill *or* ¼
  teaspoon dried dill

In a small bowl, combine all ingredients until well blended. Goes well with boiled beef, poached eggs, and vegetable salads.

Sauce Remoulade

Makes about 1⅔ cups sauce

1½ cups mayonnaise
   Yolks of 2 hard-boiled eggs,
   riced
  1 teaspoon prepared mustard
  2 small dill pickles, chopped
  1 tablespoon capers, chopped
  2 tablespoons minced mixed
   herbs
½ teaspoon anchovy paste *or*
   to taste

In a small bowl, mix mayonnaise with egg yolks and mustard. Add remaining ingredients. Serve with cold meats or fish.

Herb Dressing

Makes about ½ cup dressing

⅓ cup sour cream
⅓ cup whipping cream
  2 tablespoons minced mixed
   herbs
  3 tablespoons ketchup
   Salt
   Pepper
   Paprika

In a small bowl, combine sour cream and cream. Add herbs and ketchup; season to taste with salt, pepper and paprika. Goes especially well with cucumber salad.

Horseradish Cream

Makes 1 cup cream

2 to 3 tablespoons horseradish
1 cup whipping cream, stiffly
   beaten
   Salt
   Sugar
   Lemon juice

In a small bowl, fold horseradish into whipped cream. Season to taste with salt, sugar and lemon juice. Serve with boiled beef, ham, or smoked salmon.

Remoulade Sauce, Herb Dressing, Horseradish Cream, this page

Dill Butter

Makes ½ to ⅔ cup butter

4 ounces unsalted butter,
softened
6 tablespoons minced dill
Salt
White pepper
Thyme

In a small bowl, cream butter. Add dill and season to taste with salt, pepper and thyme. Goes well with poached or broiled fish.

Curry Butter

Makes ½ cup butter

4 ounces unsalted butter,
softened
1 tablespoon curry powder
Salt

In a small bowl, cream butter with curry powder. Season to taste with salt. Goes well with broiled chicken or fried fish.

Paprika Butter

Makes ½ cup butter

4 ounces unsalted butter,
softened
1 tablespoon paprika
Salt

In a small bowl, cream butter with paprika. Season to taste with salt. Goes well with broiled meats.

Anchovy Butter

Makes about ½ cup butter

4 ounces unsalted butter,
softened
5 anchovy fillets, finely
chopped
2 to 3 teaspoons minced onion
Anchovy paste

In a small bowl, cream butter. Add anchovy fillets and onion. Correct seasoning with anchovy paste. Goes well with fish.

Tangy Lingonberry Sauce

Makes about ⅔ cup sauce

6 tablespoons sour cream
6 tablespoons preserved
  lingonberries
2 teaspoons prepared mustard
1 teaspoon horseradish

In a small bowl, combine all ingredients well. Serve with cold beef.

Onion Butter

Makes about ½ cup butter

4 ounces unsalted butter,
  softened
4 tablespoons minced red
  onions
Salt
Pepper

In a small bowl, cream butter; add onion. Season to taste with salt and pepper. Goes well with hamburgers or roast beef.

Mustard Butter

Makes ½ cup butter

4 ounces unsalted butter,
  softened
2 teaspoons prepared mustard
  Juice of ½ lemon
  Salt

In a small bowl, cream butter with mustard; gradually add lemon juice. Season to taste with salt. Serve on steaks or burgers.

Helpful Hints

Float one or two flower blossoms in large brandy snifters for easy and elegant table decorations.

Eating Light

Pear Salad

(Illustrated previous page)
Makes 4 servings

4 medium pears, washed and dried
Lemon juice
⅔ cup yogurt
1 to 2 tablespoons sugar
⅛ teaspoon vanilla
Cinnamon
⅓ to ½ cup old-fashioned rolled oats
1 to 2 tablespoons chopped walnuts

Quarter and core pears; slice. Sprinkle with lemon juice. Reserve some slices for garnish; place remaining slices in serving bowls. In a small bowl, combine yogurt with sugar, vanilla and cinnamon to taste. Carefully fold oats and walnuts into yogurt. Spoon over fruit. Garnish with reserved pear slices.
Variations: Replace fresh pears with drained canned fruit, such as pears, peaches or cherries. Replace oats with granola or your favorite crunchy cereal, lightly crushed.

Grape Cup

Makes 2 to 3 servings

8 ounces red *or* green seedless grapes
8 ounces small curd cottage cheese
1 tablespoon lemon juice
1 to 2 tablespoons sugar
½ cup sliced blanched almonds, toasted

Remove grapes from stems. Wash, pat dry and cut in half. Combine in a medium bowl with cottage cheese, lemon juice and sugar. Fill glasses or bowls with layers of almonds and cottage cheese mixture.

Berry Foam

Makes 1 serving

1 large egg, divided
1 tablespoon sugar
4 to 6 ounces fresh raspberries, blackberries, strawberries, *or* blueberries
3 tablespoons crunchy cereal

In a serving bowl, combine egg white with sugar; beat until stiff. In a small bowl, beat egg yolk until thick and creamy; fold egg white and yolk together. Carefully fold berries and cereal into egg foam.

Tropical Breakfast

Makes 4 servings

1 mango, peeled, halved and
  pitted
2 Kiwis, peeled
2 bananas, peeled
2 nectarines *or* peaches,
  halved and pitted
1 tablespoon lemon juice
2 tablespoons sugar, optional
1 cup buttermilk
⅔ cup granola *or* crunchy
  cereal

Slice fruit and place in a glass bowl. Sprinkle with lemon juice and sugar; mix gently. Pour buttermilk over fruit and top with granola.

Endive Salad

Makes 2 servings

1 Belgian endive, trimmed and
  cored
1 medium orange, peeled
1 medium apple, diced
1 tablespoon lemon juice
2 tablespoons whipping cream
1 teaspoon sugar
  Salt
3 to 4 tablespoons crunchy
  cereal
  Parsley

Wash endive leaves; pat dry. Reserve 6 leaves; cut remaining endive crosswise into 1-inch strips. Remove white membrane from orange; section and dice. In a large bowl, combine lettuce, orange and apple. In a small bowl, mix lemon juice and cream. Add sugar and season to taste with salt. Add more sugar if needed. Fold dressing into salad ingredients. Arrange reserved endive on 2 serving plates. Fold cereal into salad and divide between plates. Garnish with parsley.
Variation: Replace cereal with toasted sliced almonds or with chopped walnuts.

Strawberry Pick-Me-Up

Makes 3 to 4 servings

1 pint strawberries, hulled
2 cups buttermilk
1½ to 2 cups milk
3 tablespoons sugar *or* to taste
¼ cup instant oatmeal, optional

Place all ingredients in a blender jar. Blend on high just until smooth. Chill. Serve in glasses.

Berries and Cream

Makes 4 servings

1½ pints fresh raspberries *or*
   strawberry halves
1 teaspoon grated lemon rind
   Sugar
½ cup whipping cream
1 tablespoon powdered sugar
4 tablespoons granola *or*
   crunchy cereal

Sprinkle berries with lemon rind; add sugar to taste. Mix. Divide berries between four individual serving dishes. Combine cream and sugar; beat until stiff peaks form. Sprinkle granola over berries; top with whipped cream.

Variation: Use yogurt or cottage cheese instead of whipped cream.

Granola Apples

Makes 4 servings

4 large firm apples
⅔ cup apple cider
¼ cinnamon stick
6 tablespoons granola

Preheat oven to 375° F. Peel and core apples. Place in ovenproof dish just large enough to hold apples. Add cider and cinnamon. Bake apples for 25 to 30 minutes or until just tender. Remove from oven and pan. Place on 4 serving dishes to cool. Reserve cider. Just before serving, fill apple cavities with granola. Spoon cider over apples or serve on the side.

Pineapple Crisp

Makes 4 servings

10 rings canned pineapple,
    drained
2 tablespoons orange
    marmalade
1 generous cup quick oats
3 tablespoons sugar
3 tablespoons chopped
    almonds
3½ tablespoons unsalted butter,
    melted
4 orange sections

Preheat oven to 375° F. Place 4 of the pineapple rings in a buttered ovenproof dish. Spread with orange marmalade. Cover with 4 more pineapple rings. Fill spaces with remaining pineapple, cut in pieces. In a small bowl, combine oats, sugar and almonds. Mix with melted butter; spread over pineapple. Bake for 10 to 12 minutes or until dish is heated through and topping is crisp. Top with orange sections. Serve warm or cold.

Fruit with Dipping Sauce
Makes 1¼ cup dip

1 cup sour cream
2½ tablespoons honey
1 tablespoon lemon juice *or* to taste
1 tablespoon toasted sesame seeds
Pinch of curry powder
Fresh fruit, cubed

In a small bowl, combine first 5 ingredients. Stir until smooth. Place bowl on a round platter. Surround with seasonal fresh fruit, speared on cocktail skewers.

Swiss Muesli
Makes 2 servings

1 apple, diced
Lemon juice
1 orange, peeled
1 banana, sliced
2 tablespoons toasted sliced almonds
1 tablespoon honey *or* 1 to 2 tablespoons sugar
1 to 1½ cups cold cereal
Milk *or* half-and-half

Sprinkle apple with lemon juice. Remove white membrane from orange; section and dice. Mix all the fruit with almonds and honey; fold in cereal. Transfer to serving bowls. Add milk or half-and-half to taste, or serve separately.

Garnished Apples
Makes 3 to 4 servings

3½ tablespoons unsalted butter at room temperature
3½ ounces blue cheese
1 tablespoon whipping cream
Salt
Ground caraway seed, optional
3 apples, quartered and cored
Lemon juice
Lettuce leaves, washed and dried
Chopped walnuts

In a small bowl, cream butter. Mash cheese with a fork; mix with whipping cream and butter until smooth. Season to taste with salt and caraway seed. Sprinkle apples with lemon juice. Arrange on a platter lined with lettuce leaves. Fill a pastry bag with the cheese mixture; pipe cheese over apple quarters. Sprinkle with chopped nuts.

Cottage Cheese Tomatoes
Makes 2 servings

2 large, round tomatoes
Pepper
Lemon juice
1 cup cottage cheese
⅔ cup chopped celery
2 teaspoons chopped dill *or* ½
teaspoon dried dill
2 to 6 shrimp, cooked
Shredded lettuce
Parsley

Make a crosscut into tomatoes; leave connected at bottom. Pull wedges slightly out; scoop out seeds. Sprinkle the inside of tomatoes with pepper and lemon juice. In a small bowl, mix cottage cheese, celery and dill. Spoon into tomatoes. Top with 1 to 3 shrimp. Arrange lettuce on 2 serving plates; sprinkle with lemon juice. Set tomatoes on lettuce. Garnish with parsley.

Avgolemono Soup
Makes 6 servings

6 cups instant *or* canned
chicken broth
1½ cups cooked rice
3 eggs
¼ cup lemon juice
Salt
Pepper
Lemon slices
Mint leaves

In a large saucepan, heat broth and rice. In a medium bowl, beat eggs with electric beater or wire whisk until frothy; add lemon juice. Still beating, add about 2 cups of the broth, a little at a time. Return mixture to pot; whisk or stir well. Season to taste with salt and pepper; chill. Garnish with thin lemon slices and mint leaves.

Leek and Potato Soup
Makes about 6 servings

1½ cups sliced leeks, white part
only
2 to 3 tablespoons butter
½ cup minced onion
4 cups instant beef broth
3 large potatoes, peeled and
quartered
1½ cups whipping cream
Salt
Pepper
Watercress *or* parsley

Wash leeks carefully. Heat butter in a stockpot; sauté leeks and onion until limp. Do not brown. Add broth and potatoes. Bring to a boil, then simmer, covered, for 25 to 30 minutes. Turn off heat. Cool soup for 15 to 20 minutes. Transfer to a blender jar or food processor; purée. Add cream. Season well with salt and pepper. Chill. Serve in individual bowls. Garnish each with watercress or parsley.

Filled Grapefruit
Makes 2 servings

1 large grapefruit, halved
⅔ cup yogurt
1 to 2 tablespoons sugar *or* to taste
1 peach, pitted and diced
¼ cup granola
2 maraschino cherries
  Mint leaves

Remove grapefruit sections; reserve shells. Separate pulp from membrane; dice pulp. Stir yogurt with sugar; fold in fruit and granola. Fill grapefruit shells. Garnish with cherries and mint leaves.

Apple Snack
Makes 2 servings

2 medium apples
⅔ cup yogurt
1 tablespoon sugar, optional
⅓ cup granola
  Chopped walnuts
  Raisins
  Cinnamon

Quarter, core and dice apples; place in serving bowl. Mix apples with yogurt, sugar and cereal. Add walnuts, raisins and cinnamon to taste.

Rice and Vegetable Salad
Makes 4 servings

2 cups cooked rice, cooled
½ cup cooked peas, drained
½ cup cooked mushrooms, sliced
1 tomato, peeled, cored, seeded and diced
¼ cup vegetable oil
2 tablespoons white wine vinegar
1 teaspoon prepared mustard
  Salt
  Pepper

Combine rice and vegetables in a bowl. In a small bowl, whisk together oil, vinegar and mustard. Season to taste with salt and pepper. Pour over rice; mix thoroughly.

Cucumber Boats

Makes 4 servings

1 to 2 cucumbers
Salt
Pepper
1 6-ounce can tuna, drained and flaked
2 hard-boiled eggs, diced
½ cup mayonnaise
Lemon juice
Lemon slices
Fresh dill
Tomato wedges

Trim ends off cucumbers. Halve cucumbers lengthwise. Cut into serving-sized pieces; scrape out seeds. Sprinkle with salt and pepper. Set in a colander to drain for about 45 minutes. Pat dry. In a small bowl, combine tuna, eggs and mayonnaise. Correct seasoning with lemon juice. Fill cucumber pieces. Garnish with lemon slices, dill and tomato wedges.

Cooked Carrot Salad

Makes 3 to 4 servings

8 carrots
1 to 2 shallots, peeled and minced
1 tablespoon chopped parsley
4 tablespoons vegetable oil
2 tablespoons white wine vinegar *or* lemon juice
Salt
Pepper

Trim, scrape and slice carrots. In a saucepan, cook in small amount of boiling water for about 8 minutes or until fork tender. Drain. Combine in a serving bowl with shallots and parsley. In a small bowl, whisk together oil and vinegar. Season to taste with salt and pepper. Fold into warm carrots. Cool.

Carrot Salad

Makes 3 to 4 servings

3 tablespoons lemon juice
2 to 3 teaspoons vegetable oil
1 to 2 teaspoons sugar
Salt
8 carrots, grated
Lettuce leaves, washed and dried

In a salad bowl, whisk together lemon juice, vegetable oil and sugar. Season to taste with salt. Mix well with carrots. Serve on a bed of lettuce.

Cucumber Boats, this page

Chicken and Avocado Salad

Makes 2 servings

1 whole chicken breast,
  skinned
  Chicken broth
1 sprig parsley
½ onion, peeled
1 large ripe avocado
  Lemon juice
1 small orange
3 tablespoons mayonnaise
2 tablespoons sour cream
  Lemon juice
  Pepper
  Lettuce leaves, washed and
  dried

Rinse chicken breast; pat dry. Place chicken bone side up in a saucepan; add chicken broth to cover. Add parsley and onion. Bring to a boil; immediately reduce heat and simmer, covered, for 20 minutes. Turn off heat. Cool, covered, for one hour. Remove chicken; debone. Trim breast halves; wrap in foil and chill. Discard bones; strain stock and reserve for another use. Peel and quarter avocado; remove pit. Dice pulp and sprinkle with lemon juice. Peel orange, including the white membrane. Remove pulp with a small, sharp knife, section by section. Dice. Cut breast halves crosswise into ½-inch slices. Place in a salad bowl; combine with avocado and orange. In a small bowl, blend mayonnaise with sour cream. Season to taste with lemon juice and pepper. Carefully fold into salad. Serve on lettuce leaves.

Marinated Mushrooms

Makes about 6 servings

2 cloves garlic, peeled
5 tablespoons olive oil
¾ cup water
¼ cup lemon juice
2 bay leaves
  Salt
  Pepper
1½ pounds small, firm mushrooms, trimmed and cleaned
1 to 2 tablespoons chopped
  parsley
  Tomato wedges
  Parsley leaves

Press garlic into oil. In a large skillet, combine oil, water, lemon juice and bay leaves. Season with salt and pepper to taste; bring to a boil. Cover; boil for 5 minutes. Add mushrooms and simmer, covered, for 7 to 10 minutes. Remove from heat. Correct seasoning with salt and pepper. Let mushrooms cool in liquid for several hours or overnight. Shortly before serving, drain mushrooms, mix with chopped parsley and arrange on individual plates. Garnish with tomato wedges and parsley leaves.

Gazpacho

Makes about 8 servings

1 clove garlic, peeled and
  quartered
1 onion, peeled and sliced
1 cucumber, sliced
3 tomatoes, peeled, halved,
  cored and seeded
1 green bell pepper, quartered
  and seeded
1 red bell pepper, quartered
  and seeded
2 tablespoons tomato paste
¼ cup red wine vinegar
¼ cup olive oil
  Pinch of thyme
2 eggs
1 cup vegetable cocktail juice
  Salt
  Pepper
  Garlic croutons
  Chopped chives

In blender or food processor, purée first 11 ingredients. Stir in vegetable juice and season to taste with salt and pepper. Chill. Garnish soup with croutons and chopped chives.

Cucumber Soup

Makes 4 servings

2 large cucumbers, peeled,
  seeded and chopped
½ cup green onions, chopped
½ clove garlic, peeled and
  minced
2 tablespoons lemon juice *or*
  white wine vinegar
1 cup chicken broth
1 cup sour cream
1 tablespoon mint leaves *or*
  minced dill
  Salt
  Pepper
  Sprigs of fresh mint *or* dill

Process first 7 ingredients in blender or food processor until smooth. Season well with salt and pepper. Chill. Garnish each serving with mint or dill sprigs.

Stuffed Grape Leaves
Makes 6 to 10 servings

30 preserved grape leaves, drained
⅓ cup long-grain rice
⅓ cup boiling water
2 large onions, peeled and chopped
½ pound ground beef
½ pound ground pork
2 tablespoons olive oil
1 tablespoon chopped mint leaves
1 tablespoon chopped dill
Salt
Pepper
Cinnamon, optional
1¼ cups hot instant chicken broth
3 to 4 tablespoons lemon juice
Yogurt, optional

Carefully unfold grape leaves; rinse in warm water and pat dry. In a saucepan, cover rice with boiling water; let stand 5 minutes. Drain well. Combine with onion, meat, olive oil, mint and dill. Season to taste with salt, pepper and cinnamon. Mix well. Place leaves on work surface, shiny side down. Place a spoonful of filling on the stalk end. Fold sides over and roll up toward leaf tip. Repeat with remaining leaves and filling. Place rolls tightly together in one layer in a large skillet, or stack in a saucepan. Add hot broth and lemon juice to just cover rolls. Bring to a boil. Weight rolls down with a plate to keep from unrolling; simmer for 35 to 40 minutes. Remove from heat; let cool in broth. Drain. May be served with yogurt.

Stuffed Apples
Makes 4 servings

4 large apples
Lemon juice
10 ounces sliced Gouda or Edam cheese
4 ounces hard salami, sliced
3 dill pickles
¼ cup whipping cream
Juice of 1 lemon
3 tablespoons vegetable oil
½ teaspoon prepared mustard
1 teaspoon ketchup
Salt, pepper and sugar

Cut a slice off top of apples; remove core. Carefully hollow out apples; dice flesh. Place apples in a bowl; sprinkle with lemon juice. Cut cheese, salami and pickles into small strips. Add to diced apples. In a small bowl, whisk cream, lemon juice and oil. Stir in mustard and ketchup; season to taste with salt, pepper and sugar. Fold into salad ingredients. Fill apple shells.

Stuffed Grape Leaves, this page

Smoked Ham with Artichoke Salad
Makes 2 servings

6 ounces Westphalian ham,
  sliced paper-thin
4 artichoke bottoms, canned
3 to 4 tablespoons olive oil
2 tablespoons lemon juice
  Salt
  Pepper
  Boston lettuce leaves,
  washed and dried
  Lemon slices
  Basil leaves *or* parsley

Arrange ham slices on a serving platter. Drain artichoke bottoms; cut into ½-inch strips. In a small bowl, whisk oil and lemon juice; season to taste with salt and pepper. Pour over artichoke bottoms and mix. Arrange lettuce leaves in a cup shape; fill with salad. Garnish with lemon slices and basil or parsley.

Oranges with Cereal
Makes 2 servings

2 small oranges, peeled
1 tablespoon honey
⅓ to ½ cup crunchy cereal
  Milk *or* half-and-half
  Chopped almonds *or*
  walnuts

Remove white membrane from oranges and section. Reserve 6 sections; dice the rest. In a small bowl, combine oranges with honey. Set aside for a few minutes. Fold cereal into oranges and accumulated juices. Add milk to taste. Sprinkle with nuts. Garnish with reserved orange sections.

Raspberry Cottage Cheese
Makes 2 servings

8 ounces small curd cottage
  cheese
  Juice of 1 lemon
2 tablespoons sugar *or* to taste
¼ cup almond slivers
1 pint fresh raspberries
  Boston lettuce leaves,
  washed and dried
  Lemon wedges

In a medium bowl, combine cottage cheese well with lemon juice and sugar. Add almonds. Carefully fold in raspberries without bruising them. Serve on lettuce leaves. Garnish with lemon wedges.

Pasta and Tuna Salad

Makes about 4 servings

2 cups elbow macaroni,
  cooked *al dente*
9½ ounces canned tuna, drained
  and flaked
¾ cup tiny peas, cooked and
  drained
½ cup diced red bell pepper
½ cup mayonnaise
½ to 1 teaspoon anchovy paste
1 tablespoon chopped parsley

In a salad bowl, mix first 4 ingredients. In a small bowl, combine mayonnaise with anchovy paste until well mixed; add parsley. Fold dressing into salad ingredients.

Fresh Peach Compote

Makes 4 servings

2 tablespoons light corn syrup
2 tablespoons frozen lemonade
  concentrate, thawed
2 tablespoons orange liqueur
3 medium peaches

Combine corn syrup, lemonade concentrate and liqueur; set aside. Peel, pit and slice peaches. Pour syrup mixture over peaches; stir thoroughly to coat. Cover and chill. Stir again before serving.

Salmon Paté

Makes 4 cups

¼ cup pitted ripe olives, sliced
¼ cup minced parsley
½ cup butter, melted
1 15-ounce can salmon,
  drained, boned and broken
  into chunks
2 tablespoons lemon juice
½ teaspoon salt
¼ teaspoon white pepper
1 cup heavy cream, chilled
  and whipped

Combine olives and parsley; set aside. Purée butter, salmon, lemon juice, salt, and pepper. Fold whipped cream into salmon mixture. Fold in olives and parsley. Pack the paté into small crocks or a tureen. Refrigerate overnight. Remove from the refrigerator 1 hour before serving. Serve with fresh bread or crackers.

Avocado and Cheese Sandwiches

Makes 4 sandwiches

1 ripe avocado, peeled
  Lemon juice
3 ounces Roquefort, crumbled
5 tablespoons butter, softened
  White pepper
4 slices dark sandwich bread
12 thin tomato slices
  Parsley *or* chives, chopped

Halve and pit avocado. Mash pulp and sprinkle with lemon juice. Mash cheese with a fork and cream with butter. Add avocado and season to taste with pepper. Spread on bread slices, leaving a few tablespoons for garnish. Arrange three overlapping tomato slices in center of each sandwich. Sprinkle parsley or chives around tomatoes. Garnish with piped-on rosettes of avocado spread.
Variation: Substitute peppergrass or watercress for parsley.

Stuffed Celery

Makes 3 to 4 servings

3 to 4 celery ribs, washed and strings removed
  Salt
  Lemon juice
4 ounces Roquefort cheese, creamed
3 to 4 tablespoons whipping cream

Cut celery into serving-size pieces. Arrange on a platter, grooved side up, and sprinkle with salt and lemon juice to taste. In a small bowl, mash cheese with a fork and gradually stir in cream until the mixture is smooth. Using a pastry bag with a star tip, pipe creamed Roquefort into celery grooves.

Melon Melba

Makes 4 servings

1 10-ounce package frozen raspberries, thawed
1 to 2 tablespoons sugar
1 teaspoon cornstarch
3 cups cubed honeydew melon

Drain raspberries; reserve juice. In a small saucepan, combine sugar and cornstarch; stir in reserved juice. Cook and stir over medium heat until thick and bubbly; cook and stir for 2 minutes more. Remove from heat; stir in berries. Cool. To serve, spoon melon into dessert dishes; top with berry sauce.

Celery Root Remoulade

Makes 4 servings

2 tablespoons lemon juice
2 celery roots
¼ cup Neufchatel cheese
¼ cup plain yogurt
1 egg yolk
1 to 2 teaspoons Dijon-style
    mustard
2 teaspoons drained capers,
    finely chopped, optional
2 green onions, thinly sliced
1 clove garlic, minced
1 teaspoon lemon juice
¼ teaspoon thyme leaves
2 tablespoons finely chopped
    fresh parsley or chives
    Butter lettuce leaves

In a large bowl, combine 8 cups of cold water and lemon juice. Peel celery roots and shred them coarsely. Add to lemon water, mix well, and set aside for 5 minutes. Drain well. In a medium bowl, blend Neufchatel and yogurt. Beat in next 7 ingredients. Add drained celery root, tossing lightly until coated with dressing. Cover and refrigerate until chilled. Sprinkle with parsley and serve on butter lettuce leaves.

Wild Rice Salad

Makes 6 servings

4 cups cooked wild rice
1½ cups diced, cooked or
    smoked chicken, turkey, or
    ham
2 cups seedless grapes, halved
    or whole
½ cup unsalted cashew nuts or
    sliced almonds
1 cup frozen cooked artichoke
    hearts, chopped
¼ cup plain yogurt
¼ cup sour half-and-half or
    Neufchatel cheese

In a medium bowl, mix all ingredients gently but thoroughly. Serve at room temperature or chilled.

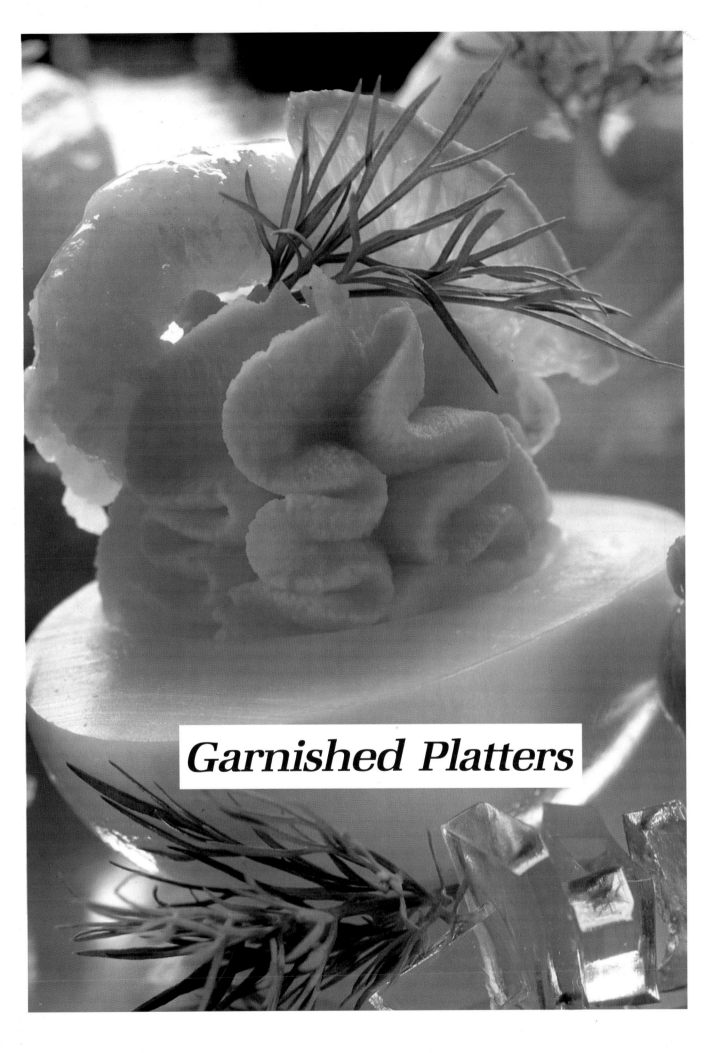

Garnished Platters

Garnished Eggs

(Illustrated previous page)
Makes 4 servings

4 hard-boiled eggs, peeled
3½ ounces French-style herb
   cream cheese
1 tablespoon whipping cream
8 cooked shrimp
   Lemon slices, quartered
   Fresh dill *or* parsley

Halve eggs lengthwise. Remove yolk and rice; place in small bowl and combine with cheese and cream. Place filling in a pastry bag fitted with a star tip; pipe into egg halves. Garnish with shrimp, lemon slices and dill.

Garnished Veal Medallions

(Illustrated previous page)
Makes 2 servings

½ pound boneless veal
   Salt
   Pepper
1 to 2 tablespoons clarified
   butter
1 tablespoon brandy
3 ounces canned liver paté
1 tablespoon whipping cream
   Diced Aspic (see page 61)
2 maraschino cherries, halved
4 mandarin orange sections
   Fresh thyme *or* mint leaves

Rinse meat; pat dry. Cut meat into 4 even slices. Season to taste with salt and pepper. Heat butter in a skillet; brown meat for 3 minutes on each side. Remove to a platter; sprinkle with brandy and cool. In a small bowl, cream liver paté with whipping cream until smooth. Spoon into pastry bag with star tip. Pipe rosettes on medallions. Garnish with aspic, cherries, orange sections and thyme.

Ham Platter

Makes 6 to 8 servings

2 pounds assorted sliced hams
½ cucumber, sliced
   Baby dill *or* gherkin fans
   Tomato wedges
   Parsley
   Assorted rolls and breads
   Butter

Arrange ham slices on a platter, overlapping them. Garnish with remaining ingredients. Serve with an assortment of rolls, breads and butter.

Saddle of Lamb in Puff Pastry

Makes 4 servings

2 **racks of lamb, about 2½ pounds each**
  Salt
  Pepper
  Thyme
4 **to 5 cloves garlic, peeled and crushed, divided**
3 **tablespoons vegetable oil**
2 **sheets frozen puff pastry, thawed**
½ **pound thinly sliced bacon**
2 **pounds spinach, washed and stems removed**
1 **egg, separated**
1 **tablespoon milk**
2 **tablespoons olive oil**
2 **tablespoons white wine vinegar**
1 **teaspoon prepared mustard**
  White wine
4 **medium tomatoes**

Bone lamb and remove fat; cut meat into 4 tenderloins. Tie 2 of the tenderloins together with kitchen string. Repeat with remaining meat. Season to taste with salt, pepper and thyme. Rub 3 cloves of garlic over meat. Heat oil in a skillet. Brown meat on all sides, about 5 minutes. Remove from heat; let cool. Remove string. Preheat oven to 400° F. On a lightly floured surface, roll each sheet of puff pastry to a rectangle large enough to cover 2 tenderloins each, about 8 x 11 inches. Place ¼ of the bacon slices side by side in the center of each pastry sheet. Place 4 spinach leaves on top of the bacon on each sheet. Place 2 tenderloins each atop the spinach. Top each with 4 more spinach leaves. Divide remaining bacon between each sheet. Brush edges of pastry with lightly beaten egg white. Fold dough over meat; press edges to seal. Transfer to a baking sheet rinsed with cold water, seam sides up. Cut 2 steam holes in top. Reroll scraps; cut into decorations. Brush with egg white and arrange on top of pastries. Lightly beat egg yolk and milk; brush over pastries. Bake for 25 to 30 minutes. Remove from oven; let cool. Transfer cooled meat to a platter. Garnish with some of the spinach leaves. Cut remaining spinach in strips; place in a bowl. Whisk together remaining garlic, olive oil, vinegar and mustard; add wine to taste. Pour over spinach. Halve tomatoes horizontally; scoop out seeds. Sprinkle with pepper. Fill with spinach salad; add to platter. Serve any remaining spinach salad separately, if desired.

Duck with Figs

Makes 2 to 3 servings

1 3-pound oven-ready duck
Salt
Pepper
Hot water
1 teaspoon unflavored gelatin
1 tablespoon cold water
1 tablespoon port
4 to 6 fresh figs
Mint leaves *or* parsley

Preheat oven to 400° F. Rinse duck; pat dry. Rub inside and out with salt and pepper to taste. Place breast side up on rack in roasting pan rinsed with water. Set in lower third of oven. During roasting, prick skin below wings and thighs from time to time to release fat. After about 30 minutes remove accumulated fat from pan. When pan juices start browning, add a little hot water. Baste duck occasionally. Add more hot water as needed. Duck should be done after about 1¾ hours. Remove from oven; cool. Strain pan juices; drain and keep hot. In a small bowl, sprinkle gelatin over cold water; set aside for 10 minutes. Stir into hot pan juices until dissolved; season juices with salt and pepper to taste. Add port and chill. Carefully remove breast meat. Slice and return to rib cage. Transfer duck to a serving platter. Make a crosscut into figs; leave connected at bottom. Lightly push sections outward. Place figs alongside duck. Cube jellied pan juices; add to platter. Garnish duck with mint or parsley.

Smoked Pork Loin Platter

Makes about 6 to 8 servings

1 3-pound boneless smoked
pork loin
Canned peach halves
Cranberry sauce
Mint leaves

Preheat oven to 375° F. Rinse meat; pat dry. Wrap in heavy-duty foil and place on middle rack in preheated oven. Bake for about 50 minutes. Remove from oven. Let rest in foil for about 15 minutes. Open foil; let meat cool. Arrange on a platter in ½-inch slices. Garnish with peach halves filled with cranberry sauce and mint leaves.

Duck with Figs, this page

Mustard Pork Roast

Makes 4 to 5 servings

1 2-pound boneless pork loin
  roast
Salt
Pepper
2 onions, peeled and minced
1 clove garlic, peeled and
  crushed
2 tablespoons hot mustard
2 tablespoons Dijon-style
  mustard
3 bunches parsley, chopped
1 teaspoon dried basil
1 teaspoon dried thyme
½ teaspoon dried sage
  Watercress
  Tomato roses
  Cocktail onions
  Marinated baby corn

Preheat oven to 400° F. Rinse meat; pat dry. Make a deep cut the length of the roast. Sprinkle with salt and pepper. In a small bowl, mix onion, garlic, mustard and herbs. Stuff into cut; spread remaining filling over top of roast. Tie meat with kitchen string. Wrap loosely in heavy-duty foil. Seal tightly. Roast on center rack for about 1½ hours. Remove from oven. Let rest in foil for 15 minutes. Open foil; let meat cool. Remove string. Slice meat and arrange on a platter. Garnish with watercress, tomato roses, cocktail onions and baby corn.

Deer Steaks in Almonds

Makes about 4 servings

4 slices leg meat, about
  ⅜-inch thick, weighing
  about 5 ounces each
Salt
Nutmeg
2 tablespoons flour
1 egg, lightly beaten
3 ounces sliced blanched
  almonds
2 to 3 tablespoons clarified
  butter
  Watercress
  Orange slices

Pound steaks lightly; season to taste with salt and nutmeg. Dredge in flour, dip in egg and coat with almonds. Press almonds into meat. In a skillet, heat butter and panfry steaks for 3 to 4 minutes on each side. Do not allow almonds to burn. Remove steaks to a serving platter; cool. Garnish with watercress and orange slices.

*Mustard Pork Roast, this
page*

Fillet of Beef with Garnishes

Makes 6 to 8 servings

4 to 5 tablespoons vegetable oil
2 2-pound center-cut beef tenderloins (Chateaubriand)
Salt
Pepper
Garnishes

Preheat oven to 425° F. In a large skillet, heat oil; brown tenderloins on all sides for about 5 minutes. Remove from heat. Season to taste with salt and pepper. Place meat in a casserole or small roasting pan. Pour skillet contents over meat. Roast for 30 minutes, turning meat several times. Baste with pan juices. Remove from oven; let cool completely. Cut each tenderloin into 14 to 16 slices. Garnish.

Garnishing Suggestions

Apricot

12 canned apricot halves
12 maraschino cherries
Mint leaves or parsley

Top 6 fillet slices with 2 apricot halves each. Place cherries in apricot hollows. Add mint or parsley. Makes 6 servings.

Mango

½ ripe mango, peeled
6 walnut halves

Cut mango into 12 thin wedges. Place 2 wedges crosswise over each of 6 fillet slices. Top with walnut halves. Makes 6 servings.

Orange

9 mandarin orange sections, drained
Chopped pistachios

Place 3 orange sections on top of each of 3 fillet slices. Sprinkle with pistachios. Makes 3 servings.

Paté

6 slices liver paté
12 mandarin orange sections, drained
Pistachios

Place paté on 6 fillet slices. Top with 2 orange sections each. Decorate with pistachios. Makes 6 servings.

Vegetable

1½ cups cooked peas
1 teaspoon unflavored gelatin
1 tablespoon cold water
⅓ cup whipping cream
⅓ cup sour cream
Salt
Pepper
Nutmeg
1 to 2 tomatoes, halved, cored and seeded
Parsley

Purée peas; force purée through a sieve. Sprinkle gelatin over cold water in a small container; let stand 10 minutes. Heat, stirring, until completely dissolved. Mix with peas. In a small bowl, whisk cream and sour cream; add to peas. Season to taste with salt, pepper and nutmeg. Spoon into a pastry bag with a star tip; pipe circles around the edges of 6 meat slices. Dice tomatoes and drain on paper towels. Spoon into pea circles. Decorate with parsley. Makes 6 servings.

Chicken Paté

1 tablespoon clarified butter
7 ounces chicken livers, washed and trimmed
Salt
Pepper
Basil
Oregano
1½ tablespoons butter, softened
Madeira *or* brandy
1 hard-boiled egg, peeled and sliced
2 to 3 stuffed olives, sliced

Heat butter in a skillet; sauté livers for about 5 minutes. Season to taste with salt, pepper and herbs; let cool. Purée and combine with butter and wine. Correct seasoning with salt and pepper. Transfer to pastry bag with star tip. Pipe rosettes over 8 fillet slices. Place an egg slice on top; garnish with an olive slice. Makes 8 servings.

Aspic

1 envelope unflavored gelatin
¼ cup cold water
¾ cup clear broth, degreased
1 to 2 tablespoons Madeira

Sprinkle gelatin over cold water. Set in a larger container with hot water until dissolved. Heat broth; remove from heat. Stir in gelatin and wine. Chill. When aspic starts to gel, brush over fillet slices. Pour remaining aspic in a shallow dish; refrigerate until firm. Cube or dice. Arrange around glazed meat on a large serving platter. Makes 8 servings.

Chef's Roulade

Makes about 6 servings

10 ounces leeks
　Boiling salted water
2 pounds boneless round steak
　Dijon-style mustard
　Salt
　Pepper
4 ounces bacon slices
1 slice white bread
14 ounces bulk bratwurst
1 egg
2 tablespoons chopped parsley
2 teaspoons green peppercorns
4 ounces chopped cooked
　mushrooms
3 tablespoons vegetable oil
2 cups red wine, divided
⅓ cup sour cream
⅓ cup whipping cream, lightly
　beaten
　Peppergrass or parsley
　Radish roses

Trim leeks removing greens to within 2½ inches of stalks. Slice leeks lengthwise. Rinse well and cook in boiling salted water for 2 to 3 minutes. Blanch and drain well. On work surface, arrange beef to form one long, thin piece of meat; pound edges together. Spread lightly with mustard. Season to taste with salt and pepper. Line meat with leeks; arrange bacon slices on top. Soak bread in cold water. Squeeze well; tear into pieces. Combine in a bowl with bratwurst, egg, parsley and green pepper. Spread over bacon layer; sprinkle with mushrooms. Roll up meat and tie at 1-inch intervals with kitchen string. Season to taste with salt and pepper. Preheat oven to 375° F. Heat oil in a casserole; brown meat on all sides. Add 1 cup of the wine, cover, and place in oven. Cook for about 1 hour, turning meat several times. Replace evaporated pan juices a little at a time with remaining wine. Transfer roulade to a platter. Cover with foil and let cool. Strain pan juices, let cool and degrease. In a shallow bowl, combine sour cream and cream. Add enough of the pan juices to make a creamy sauce. Correct seasoning with salt and pepper. Slice meat. Arrange on a serving platter with peppergrass and radishes. Serve sauce on the side.

Helpful Hints

To deglaze a pan, first degrease and then add the liquid called for. Heat and scrape bits off bottom of pan. Reduce liquid until sauce is consistency desired.

Pork Shoulder with Mint Crust

Makes 4 to 6 servings

3 pounds pork shoulder roast
Salt
Pepper
Garlic salt
3 tablespoons vegetable oil
1 cup red wine
1 cup beef broth
4 onions, peeled and quartered
2 carrots
1 clove garlic, peeled and
   crushed
1 tablespoon butter, softened
2 tablespoons mint sauce
1 tablespoon parsley, minced
1 tablespoon dill, minced
Rosemary
1 tablespoon fine bread
   crumbs
⅔ cup whipping cream
Peppermint liqueur, optional
Sprigs of dill *or* mint

Preheat oven to 350° F. Rinse meat; pat dry. Rub with salt, pepper and garlic salt to taste. Place in a roasting pan rinsed with water. Insert meat thermometer. In a small pan, heat oil; pour over meat. Place roast in oven. In a small bowl, combine wine and broth. When pan juices start to brown, add some of the liquid to pan. Baste meat from time to time with pan juices. Add more liquid as needed. Roast is done when meat thermometer registers 170° F., about 2 hours. About 30 minutes before meat is done, add onion, carrots and garlic to roasting pan. In a small bowl, about 20 minutes before meat is done, combine butter with mint sauce, parsley, dill, and rosemary to taste; add bread crumbs. Spread over meat; press well to adhere. When roast tests done, remove from oven; let cool. Deglaze pan with remaining wine and broth; reduce if necessary. Strain, cool and degrease. Stir whipping cream with enough of the pan juices to make a creamy sauce. Correct seasoning with salt and pepper. Add liqueur. Slice cold meat. Arrange on a platter; garnish with dill or mint. Serve sauce separately.

Helpful Hints

Make your own bouquet garni *by placing 6 sprigs fresh parsley, 4 celery tops, ¼ teaspoon fresh basil, 2 bay leaves, 4 peppercorns, and ¼ teaspoon thyme in a square of cheesecloth. Tie securely; use as needed. Remove once dish is cooked.*

Boiled Beef Tongue

Makes about 8 servings

1 fresh beef tongue, 4 to 5
  pounds
2 medium onions, peeled
1 clove garlic, unpeeled
2 cloves
4 to 5 sprigs parsley
1 celery rib, halved
⅛ teaspoon thyme
1 tablespoon salt
6 peppercorns
  Boston lettuce leaves,
  washed and dried
8 medium tomatoes
1 cup tiny peas, cooked
1 cup diced carrots, cooked
  Mayonnaise
4 hard-boiled eggs, peeled and
  quartered
  Pickle fans
  Parsley
  Sauce Remoulade (see page
  166) *or* Horseradish Cream
  (see page 166)

Rinse meat and pat dry. Place in stockpot or dutch oven. Add next 8 ingredients and enough water to cover meat. Bring to a boil; reduce heat and simmer, covered, for 3 to 3½ hours, or until tender. Let cool in liquid. Drain and peel off skin; discard root and gristle. Slice tongue. Arrange slices, overlapping, down the center of a large serving platter. Place lettuce leaves on both sides of meat. Cut a slice off top of each tomato; scoop out seeds. In a small bowl, mix peas and carrots with enough mayonnaise to bind; spoon into tomatoes. Arrange on lettuce with egg wedges and pickles. Garnish with parsley. Serve with Sauce Remoulade or Horseradish Cream.

Cheese Platter

Allow 6 to 8 ounces of cheese per person

Slices of Swiss, Cheddar,
Gouda, Jarlsberg cheeses
Wedges of Brie, Camembert,
Gorgonzola
Roquefort Balls (see page
86)
Seedless green grapes
Seedless red grapes
Melon balls

On a large platter, alternate overlapping slices of cheese with cheese wedges, bunches of grapes and melon balls.

Glazed Saddle of Venison

Makes 4 to 6 servings

1 3-pound saddle of venison
1 tablespoon juniper berries, crushed
1 tablespoon peppercorns, crushed
Pinch of thyme
2 bay leaves
4 cups buttermilk
1 lemon, sliced
Salt
Pepper
3 tablespoons butter, softened
½ pound thinly sliced salt pork or bacon, blanched
1 onion, peeled and quartered
Hot water
⅓ pound liver paté
2 tablespoons whipping cream
1 tablespoon basil leaves, minced or ¼ teaspoon dried basil
Asparagus tips
Seedless grapes
Kumquats
Wine Aspic (see page 68)

Rinse meat; pat dry. In a dish large enough to hold the meat, combine next 6 ingredients. Marinate meat, covered, for 2 or 3 days in refrigerator. Turn meat from time to time. Remove from marinade; pat dry. Rub with salt and pepper to taste. Spread with softened butter. Preheat oven to 400° F. Place half the salt pork slices in a roasting pan side by side. Add meat; cover with remaining pork. Place in oven. Strain marinade; remove lemon slices, reserving other seasonings. When pan juices start to brown, add reserved seasonings, onion quarters and a small amount of hot water to the pan. Baste meat from time to time. Add water as needed. Meat should be done in 45 to 60 minutes. Remove from oven. Remove meat from bones; cool and slice. In a small bowl, cream liver paté with whipping cream and basil. Spoon into a pastry bag with plain tip. Reassemble saddle; garnish with paté, asparagus spears, grapes and kumquats. Prepare Wine Aspic. As it begins to thicken, glaze saddle. Chill remaining aspic; dice into cubes and arrange on platter.

Salmon Ball

1 16-ounce can red salmon, drained
1 8-ounce package cream cheese, softened
1 small onion, finely chopped
2 tablespoons lemon juice
½ cup finely chopped parsley
¼ cup chopped nuts

Remove and discard skin and bones from salmon. Flake into a bowl. Add softened cream cheese and blend well. Add onion and lemon juice; mix well. Shape into a ball and wrap in waxed paper; refrigerate until firm. Sprinkle parsley and nuts on waxed paper; mix well. Roll salmon ball in mix until coated. Refrigerate until serving time. Place in center of platter and surround with crackers to serve.

Glazed Saddle of Venison, this page

Continental Pork and Kraut Platter

Makes 10 to 12 servings

1 2 to 3-pound smoked pork shoulder roll
1 2 to 3-pound boneless Boston-style pork shoulder roast
3 cups water
1 cup dry white wine
1 27-ounce can sauerkraut, drained
2 medium-sized tart apples, cored and cut into 8 wedges each
24 pitted prunes
3 links smoked thuringer sausage
3 links fresh bratwurst *or* knackwurst

Place smoked pork shoulder and Boston-style pork shoulder in large Dutch oven. Add water; cover tightly and simmer 2 hours. Remove meat and boil cooking liquid rapidly until it is reduced to about 2 cups. Add wine and sauerkraut, stirring to combine thoroughly. Place smoked pork shoulder and fresh pork shoulder on top of sauerkraut. Add apples, prunes, smoked thuringer and fresh bratwurst. Bring to a boil. Reduce heat and cover; simmer 30 minutes. Remove smoked and fresh pork shoulder; cool and carve in ½-inch slices. Arrange carved meat with sausage, sauerkraut and fruit on hot platter.

Salmon Steak Tartare

Makes 6 serving

3 extra large eggs, hard-boiled and chopped
1 medium onion, minced
1 pound skinned red salmon fillets, puréed
3 anchovy fillets
¼ teaspoon Tabasco sauce
¼ teaspoon Worcestershire sauce
3 tablespoons lemon juice
½ teaspoon salt
¼ teaspoon white pepper
1 medium lemon, sliced
   Minced parsley
2 medium onions, thinly sliced
   Dark bread

Combine first 9 ingredients in a large bowl; mix well. Shape salmon mixture into a ball. Cover with aluminum foil. Chill until ready to serve. Place ball on a serving platter. Surround with remaining ingredients.

Butterflied Leg Of Lamb Au Diable

Makes 6 to 8 servings

1 6 to 7-pound leg of lamb,
   boned and butterflied
1 clove garlic, crushed
½ cup salad oil
¼ cup red wine
½ cup chopped onion
2 teaspoons Dijon-style
   mustard
2 teaspoons salt
⅛ teaspoon fresh ground
   pepper
½ teaspoon oregano
½ teaspoon basil
1 bay leaf, crushed

Place the lamb fat side down in a shallow pan. Combine all seasonings and pour this marinade over the lamb. Cover pan tightly and refrigerate overnight, turning meat at least once. Take lamb out of refrigerator 1 hour before cooking. Make incisions in meat so it will lie flat. Place meat, fat side up, and marinade in broiler pan and broil 4 inches from heat for 10 minutes. Turn, baste and broil 10 minutes on the other side. Lower temperature to 425° F. and roast lamb about 15 minutes. Test with a sharp knife; meat should be pink and juicy. Remove meat from marinade and transfer to a hot platter. Bits of brown onion may be scraped off if you like. Cool and carve lamb into thin slices.

Boeuf au Gingembre

Makes 6 to 8 servings

1 4 to 5-pound eye of round
   roast
4 slices ginger root
3 slices garlic
3 tablespoons salad oil
¾ cup soy sauce
½ cup dry white wine

Make slashes in roast and tuck into each a sliver of ginger or garlic. Combine oil, soy sauce and wine. Put roast and sauce into a sealable plastic bag; refrigerate overnight. Remove roast from bag and place in a greased shallow roasting pan. Place in a preheated 450° F. oven for 30 minutes (45 minutes for a larger roast). Turn off heat, leaving roast in the oven for an additional 20 minutes. Remove from oven and let stand 10 minutes before slicing.

Helpful Hints

When choosing a meat recipe, allow ⅓ to ½ pound per serving if meat is boneless, ¾ to 1 pound if bone-in.

Desserts

Piquant Berry Salad

(Illustrated previous page)
Makes about 4 servings

1½ pounds mixed berries,
   washed and drained
   Powdered sugar, sifted
⅓ cup sour cream
⅓ cup whipping cream
1 teaspoon prepared mustard
1 tablespoon lemon juice
1 to 2 tablespoons superfine
   sugar
   Salt
   White pepper
   Grated rind of 1 orange

Place berries in a serving bowl. Lightly dust with powdered sugar. In a small bowl, mix sour cream, cream, mustard, lemon juice and sugar. Season to taste with salt and pepper; sprinkle with orange rind. Spoon on top of berries or serve on the side.

Fruity Ice Cream Cup

Makes 1 serving

1 scoop each: lemon ice
   cream, raspberry sherbet
   and peach ice cream
   Sweetened whipped cream
   Chocolate curls
   Raspberries
   Sliced peaches
1 rolled wafer

Arrange scoops in a chilled stemmed glass or dish. Top with a whipped cream rosette. Garnish with remaining ingredients.

Viennese Berries and Milk

Makes about 5 servings

1½ pounds prepared mixed
   berries
1 cup powdered sugar, sifted
2 tablespoons lemon juice
1 tablespoon orange liqueur
   Pinch of cinnamon, optional
4 cups buttermilk
   Vanilla ice cream

Carefully mix fruit with sugar, lemon juice, liqueur and cinnamon. Let stand, covered, 30 minutes. Fold in buttermilk. Serve in individual bowls with a scoop of vanilla ice cream.

Rum Cream

Makes 5 to 6 servings

1 3-ounce package instant vanilla pudding
1 cup milk
1½ cups whipping cream, divided
¼ cup dark rum
3 ounces milk chocolate, chopped
1 to 2 tablespoons powdered sugar
Maraschino cherries
Shaved chocolate

In a medium bowl, combine pudding powder, milk and ½ cup whipping cream. Whisk until smooth. Whisk in rum. Stir in chopped chocolate. In a small bowl, whip remaining cream with the powdered sugar until stiff peaks form. Reserve a few tablespoons for garnish. Fold remaining cream into pudding. Transfer to serving bowl. Garnish with rosettes of whipped cream, maraschino cherries and chocolate.

Berries and Sour Cream

Makes 4 servings

1 16-ounce package frozen raspberries, thawed
1 tablespoon unflavored gelatin
3 tablespoons cold water
2 to 3 tablespoons sugar
1¼ cups sour cream
Sweetened whipped cream
Fresh raspberries

Drain berries; reserve syrup. Set aside. In a small bowl, sprinkle gelatin over cold water; let stand 10 minutes. In a small saucepan, heat ¼ cup of the reserved syrup. Add sugar and gelatin; stir until dissolved. Set aside. Force raspberries through a sieve. Stir into sour cream with remaining syrup and gelatin. Mix well. Pour into serving bowl; refrigerate until set. Decorate with whipped cream rosettes and fresh berries.

Coffee Break

Makes 4 servings

½ cup chocolate sauce
Coffee ice cream
Sweetened whipped cream
Chocolate curls

Divide chocolate sauce between 4 chilled dessert plates. Top each with 2 to 3 scoops coffee ice cream. Garnish with whipped cream rosettes and chocolate curls.

Sherry Charlotte

Makes 4 servings

2 heaping teaspoons unflav-
    ored gelatin
3 tablespoons cold water
16 ladyfingers, preferably
    homemade
½ cup sherry, divided
3 egg yolks
⅓ cup sugar
½ teaspoon vanilla
1 tablespoon orange juice
1½ cups whipping cream
    Maraschino cherries *or* fresh
    dark cherries
    Thin strips of orange peel

In a small pan, sprinkle gelatin over cold water; let stand 10 minutes. Heat, stirring, until completely dissolved. Set aside. Place ladyfingers on a plate; sprinkle with ¼ cup sherry. Cover and set aside. In a double boiler over simmering water, beat egg yolks, sugar, vanilla and orange juice with an electric beater until thick and creamy. Remove from heat; continue beating until cooled. Add remaining sherry and luke-warm gelatin. Beat whipping cream until stiff peaks form; fold into egg and gelatin mixture. Chill. Stand 4 ladyfingers on the sides of each of 4 individual glass bowls. Fill bowls with sherry cream. Decorate with cherries and orange peel.

Fruit Salad with Orange Cream Sauce

Makes 4 to 6 servings

2 bananas, peeled and sliced
2 apples, peeled, quartered,
    cored and sliced
2 tablespoons lemon juice
1 cup red and green seedless
    grapes, halved
2 oranges, peeled, white mem-
    brane removed
4 apricots, pitted and cut into
    sections
2 tablespoons superfine sugar
⅓ cup sour cream
⅓ cup whipping cream
2 to 3 tablespoons orange li-
    queur
2 tablespoons chopped
    hazelnuts

Combine bananas and apples; sprinkle with lemon juice. Add grapes. Section oranges; cut sections in half and add to salad together with apricots. Mix with sugar and transfer to serving bowl. In a small bowl, stir sour cream, cream and liqueur. Add hazelnuts. Pour sauce over fruit salad.

Sherry Charlotte, this page

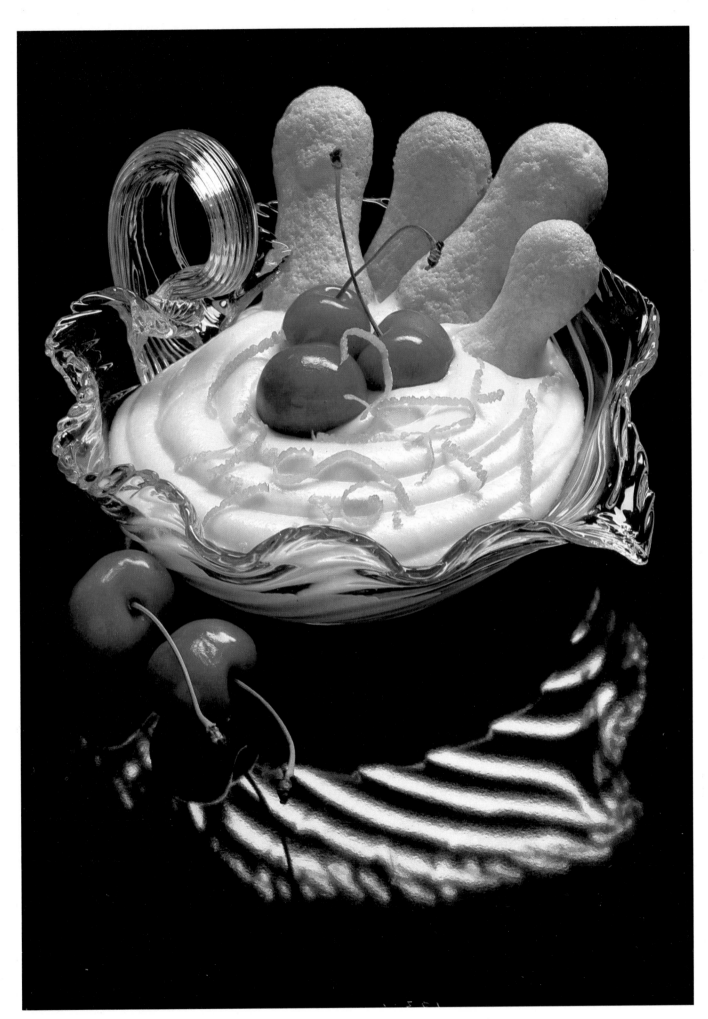

Orange Walnut Cream

Makes 4 to 5 servings

1 envelope unflavored gelatin
¼ cup cold water
2 eggs, separated
2 tablespoons warm water
3 tablespoons sugar
1 cup orange juice
½ cup milk
2 tablespoons orange liqueur
1 cup whipping cream
3 ounces chopped walnuts
    Walnut halves

In a small pan, sprinkle gelatin over cold water; let stand 10 minutes. Heat, stirring, until gelatin is completely dissolved. With an electric hand beater, beat egg yolks and warm water until foamy. Gradually add sugar and continue beating until creamy. Beat in orange juice, milk, liqueur and the lukewarm gelatin mixture. Chill. In separate bowls, stiffly beat egg whites and whipping cream. Reserve some whipped cream for decoration. When orange cream starts to thicken, fold in whipped cream and egg whites. Add chopped walnuts. Transfer cream to a serving bowl or individual dessert dishes; chill. Before serving, decorate with remaining whipped cream and walnut halves.

Blueberry Bavarian

Makes about 6 servings

2 envelopes unflavored gelatin
½ cup cold water
1½ pounds blueberries, washed
    and drained
1¾ cups powdered sugar
    Lemon juice
6 egg yolks
2 tablespoons lukewarm water
2 cups whipping cream

In a small saucepan, stir gelatin into cold water; let stand 10 minutes. Heat, stirring, until dissolved. Purée a little more than half the blueberries with half the powdered sugar. Add lemon juice and gelatin. In a small bowl, with electric beater, beat egg yolks and lukewarm water until foamy. Gradually add remaining powdered sugar. Stir into puréed blueberries. In a medium bowl, whip cream until stiff. When blueberry mixture starts to thicken, fold berries and whipped cream together. Spoon into a 1-quart mold, rinsed with cold water. Chill. When Bavarian is completely set, unmold onto a serving platter. May be garnished with additional, sweetened whipped cream.

Baked Custard with Blackberry Sauce

Makes 6 servings

3 eggs
⅓ cup sugar
Salt
2½ cups milk, scalded
½ teaspoon vanilla
¾ teaspoon grated lemon peel, divided
1 17-ounce can blackberries
2 teaspoons cornstarch
1 teaspoon brandy, optional

Preheat oven to 350° F. In a bowl, combine eggs, sugar, and ¼ teaspoon salt; beat until light-colored. Gradually blend in milk, vanilla, and ½ teaspoon lemon peel. Pour into six 6-ounce custard cups. Place cups in a 13 x 9-inch baking dish. Fill with ½ inch hot water. Bake for 35 to 40 minutes or until a knife inserted near the center comes out clean. Cool to room temperature. Refrigerate until chilled. Drain the blackberries, reserving syrup. In a saucepan, combine cornstarch, remaining ¼ teaspoon lemon peel, and a dash of salt. Gradually add the reserved syrup; blend until smooth. Cook over medium heat, stirring constantly until thickened. Stir in brandy. Allow the sauce to cool, then stir in the blackberries. Refrigerate until chilled. Unmold custard into serving dishes. Top with blackberry sauce.

Lemon Torte

Makes 12 servings

1 large *or* 1½ small angel food cakes
1 tablespoon unflavored gelatin
¼ cup cold water
6 egg yolks
1½ cups sugar, divided
⅔ cup lemon juice
2 teaspoons grated lemon rind
6 egg whites
1 pint whipping cream, whipped
Shredded coconut, optional

Trim brown crusts from cake and cut cake into cubes. Soften gelatin in cold water. Combine egg yolks, ¾ cup sugar, lemon juice and rind. Cook over hot (not boiling) water. Stir until mixture coats spoon. Remove from heat and add gelatin, stirring until dissolved. Cook until partially thickened. Beat egg whites, gradually adding remaining sugar. Beat until stiff. Fold into custard and mix with cake cubes. Pour into a lightly oiled torte pan or large bowl and refrigerate overnight. Remove from pan and frost with whipped cream. Sprinkle with coconut if desired.

Black Forest Cream

Makes 4 to 5 servings

1 3-ounce package instant
  French vanilla pudding
1⅓ cups milk
2 tablespoons kirsch
1 cup whipping cream
1 tablespoon powdered sugar
1 can sour cherries, drained
  Shaved chocolate
  Wafer cookies

In a medium bowl, combine pudding powder, milk and kirsch. Whisk until smooth. Set aside. Whip cream and powdered sugar until stiff. Reserve a few tablespoons for decoration. Fold remaining cream into pudding. Chill. Fill individual bowls or stemmed glasses with alternating layers of cherries and cream; end with cream. Garnish with reserved whipped cream and shaved chocolate. Serve with cookies. *Variation*: Substitute chocolate pudding for vanilla.

Cinnamon Parfait

Makes about 6 servings

8 ounces pitted prunes
3½ cups water, divided
3 eggs, separated
½ cup sugar, divided
1 teaspoon cinnamon
3 tablespoons brandy
2 cups whipping cream
2 oranges
  Shaved chocolate

Place prunes in a medium saucepan; cover with 3 cups water. Bring to a boil; simmer for 20 minutes. Drain. With electric beater, beat egg yolks and ¼ cup sugar until foamy. Beat in cinnamon and brandy; set aside. Stir together the egg whites and 1 tablespoon sugar. Beat until stiff. Set aside. Whip cream until stiff peaks form. Fold into yolk mixture. Fold in egg whites. Transfer to a freezer bowl, cover and freeze for about 12 hours. Thinly strip orange peel; cut into fine strips. Cook in a small saucepan with remaining ½ cup water and 3 tablespoons sugar until syrupy. Cool. Remove remaining peel from oranges. Separate sections from membrane. Shortly before serving, place scoops of parfait on individual serving plates. Arrange prunes and orange sections around ice cream. Glaze fruit with syrup. Decorate with shaved chocolate.

Cinnamon Parfait, this page

Cardinal Peaches

Makes 1 serving

3 scoops butter pecan ice
cream
Sweetened whipped cream
1 canned peach half, drained
Raspberry Sauce (recipe
below)
Chopped pecans

Place ice cream in an individual serving
dish or stemmed glass. Garnish with
whipped cream. Add peach half and top
with Raspberry Sauce. Sprinkle with
chopped pecans.

Raspberry Sauce

1 10-ounce package frozen
raspberries
3 tablespoons currant jelly
1 tablespoon lemon juice

Partially thaw raspberries. Place in blender
jar with remaining ingredients; blend until
smooth. Strain.

Nectarine Cream

Makes 4 servings

2 teaspoons unflavored gelatin
2 tablespoons cold water
1 pound nectarines, halved
and pitted
1½ cups white wine
¼ cup sugar
1 cup whipping cream

In a small pan, sprinkle gelatin over cold
water; let stand 10 minutes. Heat, stirring,
until dissolved. Dice nectarines. Place in a
medium saucepan with 1 cup wine and
sugar. Poach fruit for about 8 minutes. Remove from heat. Remove nectarines with a
slotted spoon. Set about one quarter of
them aside; purée the remaining fruit. Return to saucepan; add enough wine to
make 2 cups. Stir in gelatin. Whip cream
until stiff peaks form. Reserve a few tablespoons for garnish. When nectarine mixture begins to thicken, fold in whipped
cream and diced fruit. Spoon into dessert
glasses; garnish with whipped cream.

Melba Cup
Makes 1 serving

2 to 3 scoops strawberry ice
    cream
½ peach, sliced *or* canned
    sliced peaches, drained
    Lemon juice
    Strawberry Sauce (recipe
    below)
    Sweetened whipped cream

Place ice cream scoops on serving plate. Sprinkle peach slices with lemon juice; arrange over ice cream. Top with Strawberry Sauce. Garnish with whipped cream rosettes.

Strawberry Sauce

1 10-ounce package frozen
    strawberries
3 tablespoons currant jelly
1 teaspoon lemon juice

Thaw strawberries partially. Place in blender jar with remaining ingredients; blend until smooth.

Chocolate Mousse
Makes about 4 servings

5 ounces semisweet or bitter-
    sweet chocolate, chopped
3 eggs, separated
1 whole egg
2 generous tablespoons sugar
2 tablespoons coffee liqueur
1 teaspoon instant coffee
    powder
⅔ cup whipping cream

Place chocolate in top of small double boiler over simmering water. Stir until melted. Remove from heat. In top of large double boiler, combine 3 egg yolks, egg, sugar, liqueur and coffee powder. Beat with electric beater for 5 to 7 minutes until foamy. Remove from steam; beat about 5 minutes more until cold. Beat egg whites until stiff. Beat whipping cream until stiff. Stir melted chocolate into egg yolk mixture. Fold in whipped cream and egg whites. Spoon into individual serving dishes. Serve well chilled.

Raspberry Mold

Makes 4 to 5 servings

1 3-ounce package raspberry
   gelatin
1 cup boiling water
½ cup cold water
¼ cup white wine
1 tablespoon lemon juice
1½ cups fresh raspberries
   Sweetened whipped cream
   Vanilla sauce (recipe below)

In a medium saucepan, dissolve gelatin in boiling water. Add cold water, wine and lemon juice. Rinse a 3-cup mold with cold water. Pour a thin layer of gelatin in bottom; chill until set. Set pan with remaining gelatin in ice water to cool. Set aside about ¼ cup raspberries for decoration. Add remaining berries to mold. When gelatin starts to thicken, add to mold. Chill for 4 hours or more. To unmold, loosen edges with a small knife. Dip mold very briefly in hot water; invert onto serving plate. Decorate with rosettes of whipped cream and reserved berries. Top with vanilla sauce or serve sauce separately.

Vanilla Sauce

Makes 1¼ cups sauce

1 cup milk
4 egg yolks
½ cup sugar
¼ teaspoon vanilla

In a small saucepan, bring milk to a boil; cover and set aside. In a small bowl, beat egg yolks, sugar and vanilla with electric beater until thick and creamy. Slowly stir in milk (do not beat). Return mixture to saucepan and cook over low heat, stirring, until sauce coats a spoon. Do not boil. Remove from heat and set in a pan with ice water. Stir until cold.

Double Strawberry Yogurt

Makes 2 servings

1 pint fresh strawberries,
   washed and hulled
   Lemon juice
2 teaspoons sugar
⅔ cup strawberry yogurt

Reserve 2 strawberries for garnish. Halve or quarter remaining berries. Sprinkle with lemon juice and sugar; mix. Fold into yogurt. Transfer to 2 individual serving bowls. Garnish with reserved berries and serve.

Raspberry Mold, this page

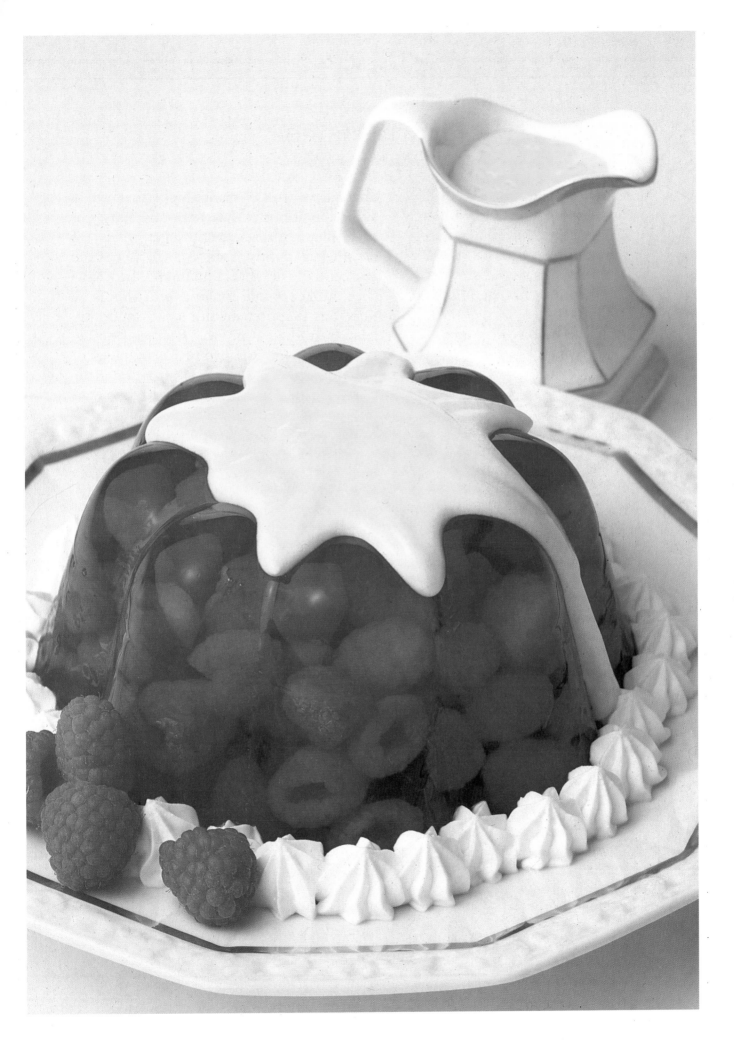

Kiwis Flambé

Makes 4 servings

4 Kiwis, peeled
2 tablespoons unsalted butter
2 tablespoons sliced blanched almonds
2 tablespoons sugar
2 tablespoons orange juice
Cinnamon
¼ cup Calvados *or* brandy
Ice cream

Slice Kiwi fruit ¼-inch thick. In a small skillet, melt butter. Add almonds; toast until golden. Sprinkle with sugar; allow to caramelize lightly. Add orange juice and season to taste with cinnamon. Add Kiwi slices and continue cooking until almost all juice has evaporated. In a small saucepan, heat Calvados. Pour over fruit and ignite. Place scoops or squares of ice cream on 4 individual serving plates. Divide hot Kiwi slices over ice cream.

Chilled Strawberries with Lemon Cream

Makes 4 servings

2 pints strawberries, washed and hulled
Sugar
Crushed ice
1 cup whipping cream
4 to 6 tablespoons powdered sugar
2 tablespoons lemon juice

Slice strawberries thickly. Layer in a serving bowl. Sprinkle each layer with sugar to taste. Place in a larger bowl filled with crushed ice. Whip cream for about 1 minute. Mix powdered sugar and cream. Continue whipping until stiff peaks form. Carefully fold in lemon juice. Serve berries and cream separately.

Molded Cherry Ice Cream

Makes about 6 servings

1 quart black cherry ice cream, slightly softened
1 cup whipping cream
2 tablespoons powdered sugar
1 tablespoon kirsch
Cherries
Wafer cookies

Transfer ice cream to an oval 1-quart mold. Refreeze until firm. In a small bowl, whip cream and sugar until stiff peaks form; add kirsch. Spoon into a pastry bag with star tip. Invert ice cream mold onto an oval platter. Cup with warm hands or cover briefly with a warm damp towel; remove mold. Pipe whipped cream rosettes around molded ice cream. Decorate with cherries. Serve with wafer cookies.

Pear Charlotte

Makes 6 servings

Butter
Ladyfingers
1 envelope unflavored gelatin
¼ cup cold water
1 3-ounce package instant
  chocolate pudding
1⅔ cups milk
1 cup whipping cream
3 canned pear halves, cut into
  wedges
Shaved chocolate

Butter an 8-inch springform pan; line with waxed paper. Line bottom and sides of pan with split ladyfingers, curved side out. In a small pan, sprinkle gelatin over cold water; let stand 10 minutes. Heat, stirring, until gelatin is dissolved. Prepare pudding according to package directions; stir in gelatin. In a small bowl, whip cream until stiff; fold into pudding as soon as it begins to thicken. Place pear in bottom of pan in sunburst pattern. Pour pudding into pan. Chill. Remove from pan and sprinkle with shaved chocolate.

Grapes on Ice

Makes 4 servings

½ pound Ribier grapes, washed
½ pound green seedless grapes
2 to 3 tablespoons sugar
Crushed ice
¼ cup Framboise

Remove washed grapes from stems. Cut in half; remove seeds in Ribier grapes. Place in a bowl and sprinkle with sugar. Put a layer of crushed ice in each of 4 individual serving bowls. Divide grapes between bowls; add 1 tablespoon Framboise each.

Ice Cream Cup Helena

Makes 1 serving

2 to 3 scoops pistachio ice
  cream
2 to 3 canned apricot halves,
  drained
Strawberry Sauce (see page 217)
Sweetened whipped cream
Toasted sliced almonds
Rolled waffle cookies

Place ice cream on chilled plate. Top each scoop with an apricot half. Pour strawberry sauce over apricots. Garnish with whipped cream and almonds. Serve with cookies.

Walnut Cream

Makes 4 servings

1 envelope unflavored gelatin
⅓ cup cold water
2 eggs, separated
1 tablespoon hot water
⅓ cup sugar
½ teaspoon vanilla
⅓ cup Advocat liqueur *or* eggnog
2 ounces ground walnuts
1 cup whipping cream
   Walnut halves

In a small pan, sprinkle gelatin over cold water; let stand 10 minutes. With electric beater, whip yolks and hot water until foamy. Add sugar gradually. Stir in vanilla and liqueur. Add ground nuts. Heat gelatin, stirring, until dissolved. Add 3 tablespoons of the egg mixture; stir well. Beat into remaining egg mixture. If too soft, chill. Beat egg whites until stiff. Beat whipping cream until stiff. Reserve a few tablespoons of whipped cream for garnish. When egg mixture begins to thicken, fold in whipped cream and egg whites. Spoon into stemmed glasses; chill. Decorate with reserved whipped cream and walnut halves.

Vanilla Cream and Wine Foam

Makes 5 to 6 servings

Generous ¼ cup cornstarch, divided
⅜ cup sugar, divided
2 cups milk, divided
½ teaspoon vanilla, *or* to taste
2 eggs, separated
1 whole egg
1 cup white wine
   Grated rind of ½ lemon
1 tablespoon lemon juice

In a measuring cup, combine cornstarch, except for 1 generous tablespoon, with 2 tablespoons sugar. Stir in 6 tablespoons of milk. In a medium saucepan, bring remaining milk to a boil. Remove from heat; stir in cornstarch mixture and vanilla. Return to heat; bring to a boil, stirring; cook for about 2 minutes, stirring continuously. Set aside to cool. In a small bowl, beat 2 egg whites until stiff; fold into cooled cream. Transfer to a serving bowl. Bowl should be about half full. In a small saucepan, combine 2 egg yolks, whole egg, remaining corn starch, remaining sugar, wine, lemon rind and juice. Set in a larger pan with simmering water. Beat with a wire whisk until a large bubble rises (about 20 minutes). Do not boil. Let cool. Pour wine foam over cream. Serve immediately.

Walnut Cream, this page

Brandied Apricots
Makes 8 servings

8 ripe apricots
6 tablespoons sugar
6 tablespoons brandy
½ to 1 cup whipping cream
1 to 3 tablespoons powdered
    sugar, *or* to taste

Wash and dry apricots. Prick several times with a toothpick or fork. Place in a bowl, sprinkle with sugar and brandy; cover and set aside. Turn fruit from time to time. Remove apricots to 8 individual serving plates. Transfer juices to a small saucepan. Heat, stirring; bring to a boil. Pour over fruit; let cool. Whip cream and sugar until stiff. Pipe over apricots.

Ice Cream Cup Alexandria
Makes 1 serving

Walnut ice cream
1 to 2 tablespoons eggnog
  Sweetened whipped cream
  Walnut halves
  Chopped pistachios

Place 2 or 3 scoops of ice cream in individual stemmed dishes. Add eggnog. Garnish with whipped cream rosettes, walnut halves and chopped pistachios.

Cherry Cream
Makes about 6 servings

2 egg yolks
3 to 4 tablespoons sugar
3 tablespoons cherry liqueur
1 envelope unflavored gelatin
3 tablespoons cold water
2 cups whipping cream
2 tablespoons powdered sugar
  Ladyfingers
  Cherries
  Shaved chocolate

With electric beater, beat egg yolks until foamy. Add sugar gradually and continue beating until thick and creamy. Add liqueur. In a small pan, sprinkle gelatin over cold water; let stand 10 minutes. Heat, stirring, until completely dissolved. Set aside. In a large bowl, whip cream until it starts to thicken. Add sugar and continue beating until almost stiff. Pour cooled (but not thickened) gelatin over the whipped cream; beat until stiff. Fold into egg mixture. Line a serving bowl with ladyfingers; fill with cream. Decorate with cherries and shaved chocolate. Serve very cold or semi-frozen.

Berries in Champagne Zabaglione

Makes 4 to 5 servings

8 ounces prepared raspberries
8 ounces prepared blackberries
3 tablespoons sugar, divided
2 egg yolks
1 egg
1 tablespoon lemon juice
1 cup champagne, divided

Reserve a few berries for garnish. Divide remaining berries between 4 to 5 individual dessert glasses; sprinkle with 1 tablespoon sugar. In top of double boiler over simmering water, beat egg yolks, egg, remaining sugar, lemon juice and ½ cup champagne with electric beater until creamy (about 7 minutes). Pour remaining ½ cup champagne over fruit. Top with zabaglione. Decorate with reserved berries.

Pistachio Cup

Makes 4 servings

1 mango, peeled, halved and
   pitted
2 tablespoons Grand Marnier
8 scoops pistachio ice cream
   Sweetened whipped cream

Cube mango. Place in a small bowl and sprinkle with liqueur. Let stand 15 to 20 minutes. Place 2 scoops of ice cream in 4 individual bowls; arrange mango around ice cream. Decorate with rosettes of whipped cream.

Banana and Ginger Ice Cream

Makes about 5 servings

3 bananas, peeled and mashed
2 egg yolks
2 tablespoons honey
⅓ cup lemon juice
3 tablespoons chopped preserved ginger
1 cup whipping cream
   Chocolate sauce

Whip bananas, egg yolks, honey and lemon juice until fluffy. Stir in ginger. Whip cream until stiff peaks form; fold into banana mixture. Transfer to ice cube trays. Freeze. Just before serving, cube ice cream; place in dessert glasses. Top with chocolate sauce or serve sauce separately. Serve at once.

Zabaglione

Makes 4 servings

4 egg yolks
¼ cup sugar
½ cup Marsala
   Almond macaroons

In top of double boiler over simmering water, beat yolks and sugar with electric beater until thick and creamy. Add Marsala. Continue beating until thick and fluffy. Immediately pour into stemmed glasses. Garnish with almond macaroons.

Mixed Fruit with Orange Sauce

Makes 4 servings

2 apples, peeled, quartered
   and cored
2 oranges, peeled and sectioned
1 Kiwi, peeled
1 banana, peeled
4 strawberries, washed, hulled
   and halved
1 cup seedless grapes
2 tablespoons sugar, optional
⅔ cup whipping cream
2 tablespoons orange liqueur
   Chopped hazelnuts

Dice apples and oranges. Slice Kiwi and bananas. Quarter Kiwi slices. Combine in a bowl with strawberries and grapes. Sprinkle with sugar. In a small bowl, whip cream until soft peaks form. Stir in orange liqueur. Spoon fruit into individual dessert glasses. Top with orange sauce and sprinkle with hazelnuts.

Berries with Strawberry Cream

Makes 4 servings

½ cup each prepared blueberries, red currants, blackberries, and raspberries
1 to 2 tablespoons sugar
½ cup prepared strawberries,
   quartered
¾ cup whipping cream
1 to 2 tablespoons powdered
   sugar
1 tablespoon Framboise

Combine blueberries, currants, blackberries and raspberries in serving bowl. Sprinkle with sugar. Cut strawberry quarters in half. Whip cream and powdered sugar to soft peaks. Stir in Framboise. Fold in strawberries. Distribute over berries.

Zabaglione, this page

Ice Cream with Orange Eggnog Topping

Makes 6 servings

3 oranges
3 to 4 tablespoons Grand Marnier
Half of ½ gallon brick vanilla ice cream
1½ cups eggnog
Almond slivers
Shaved chocolate

Peel oranges, including the white membrane; slice thinly. Sprinkle with liqueur; set aside to steep. Cut ice cream into 12 rectangular pieces. Arrange on 6 individual serving plates. Distribute orange slices and their liquid over ice cream; top with eggnog. Sprinkle with almonds and chocolate.

Blackberry Ice Cream Cup

Makes 4 servings

1½ pints prepared blackberries
2 to 3 tablespoons sugar
Vanilla ice cream
Sweetened whipped cream

Reserve a few blackberries for garnish. Place the remaining berries in a bowl; sprinkle with sugar. Let stand until some juice has accumulated. Transfer berries and juice to 4 chilled dessert glasses. Add 2 to 3 scoops ice cream to each glass; top with whipped cream rosettes. Decorate with reserved berries.

Fresh Fruit Gelati

Makes 4 servings

2 ripe bananas
2 ripe papayas
1 tablespoon orange juice
1 tablespoon lemon juice
1 tablespoon lime juice
1 tablespoon grated orange rind
1 tablespoon grated lemon rind
1 tablespoon grated lime rind
4 cups milk
½ cup sugar
1 teaspoon vanilla

Combine all ingredients in food processor. Process until blended. Transfer to shallow cake pan and freeze overnight. Process again until smooth. Transfer to bowl and freeze overnight again.

Melon and Fruit Salad

Makes 4 to 5 servings

1 small honeydew melon,
  quartered and seeded
2 apples, peeled, quartered
  and cored
2 bananas, peeled and sliced
1 11-ounce can mandarin
  oranges, drained
2 to 3 tablespoons lemon juice
2 tablespoons honey
  Chopped almonds

Thinly slice melon and apples. Combine in a bowl with banana slices and orange sections. Stir lemon juice into honey; mix well. Fold into fruit salad. Transfer to serving bowl. Sprinkle with chopped almonds.

Red Wine Cream

Makes 4 to 5 servings

1 3-ounce package raspberry
  gelatin
1 cup boiling water
¾ cup red wine
1 cup whipping cream
1 tablespoon powdered sugar

Dissolve gelatin in boiling water. Add wine; cool. In a small bowl, whip cream and sugar until stiff. Reserve a few tablespoons for garnish. Fold remaining cream into slightly thickened gelatin. Transfer to serving bowl or to individual bowls. Garnish with reserved whipped cream.

Bananas with Rum Cream

Makes 4 servings

1 egg, separated
¼ cup brown sugar
1 tablespoon dark rum
½ of 4-ounce container frozen
  whipped dessert topping,
  thawed
4 small bananas, sliced
  Chocolate curls, optional

In a small mixer bowl, beat egg white until soft peaks form; gradually add half of the brown sugar, beating until stiff peaks form. Transfer to a clean bowl. In the same mixer bowl, beat egg yolk until thick and lemon colored; beat in remaining brown sugar and rum. Fold egg white and dessert topping into yolk mixture. Chill until serving time. To serve, place sliced bananas in 4 dessert dishes. Spoon rum cream over fruit. Garnish with chocolate curls, if desired.

Ice Cream and Pears

Makes 6 servings

½ gallon brick vanilla ice
   cream
1 ounce semisweet *or* bitter-
   sweet chocolate
½ cup whipping cream
6 canned pear halves, drained
3 tablespoons pear brandy
   Shaved chocolate
   Wafer cookies

Slice ice cream into 12 even rectangles. Keep frozen. In a double boiler, melt chocolate over hot water, stirring. In a small bowl, whip cream until stiff. Fold chocolate into cream. Spoon into pastry bag. Arrange ice cream slices on 6 serving dishes. Add 1 pear half to each; sprinkle with brandy. Pipe chocolate cream over pears. Decorate with shaved chocolate. Serve with wafer cookies.

Chocolate Pots-de-Creme

Makes 4 servings

2 cups whole milk *or* 1 cup
   each milk and half-and-half
6 ounces grated chocolate
6 egg yolks, lightly beaten
1 teaspoon vanilla *or* grated
   rind of 1 orange *or* 1 tablespoon *each* instant
   coffee and cognac

Stir milk and chocolate in a medium saucepan over medium heat until blended and scalded. Remove from heat; beat in eggs and vanilla. Strain and pour into 4 dainty serving cups. Chill.

Peaches and Cream

Makes about 4 servings

4 medium-size ripe peaches
2 tablespoons sugar
2 tablespoons dark rum
¾ cup whipping cream
1 to 2 tablespoons powdered
   sugar

Halve and pit peaches; slice. Arrange slices in a glass serving bowl. Sprinkle with sugar and rum. In a small bowl, whip cream with powdered sugar until stiff peaks form. Fold into peaches.

Ice Cream and Pears,
this page

Cold Soufflé Cordon Bleu

Makes 4 servings

1 cup milk
½ vanilla pod, split, *or* 1 to 2
   teaspoons vanilla
6 eggs, separated
½ to 1 cup sugar
1 envelope unflavored gelatin
¼ cup Cointreau, rum, *or*
   Grand Marnier
1 teaspoon grated orange rind
1 teaspoon grated lemon rind
1 cup whipping cream
2 tablespoons powdered sugar
6 to 8 shortbread cookies
   Additional Cointreau
   Mint leaves, fresh berries,
   citrus slices, *or* candied
   violets

Tie a band of greased foil around a soufflé dish; lightly oil a jam jar and place it in the center of the soufflé dish. Place a mixing bowl in the freezer. Scald milk with vanilla pod. Discard pod. Beat egg yolks with sugar until thick. Slowly pour hot milk into yolks, beating continually. Return to pan; cook over low heat until custard thickens and becomes creamy. Strain immediately into the cold mixing bowl and return to freezer. Soak and dissolve gelatin in liqueur over low heat. Add to custard with orange and lemon rind; mix thoroughly. Place in refrigerator until mixture is partially set. Beat egg whites until stiff. Beat cream and powdered sugar until stiff. Fold ½ of the whipped cream and all of the beaten egg whites into the custard. Pour quickly into soufflé dish around jam jar. Refrigerate until set. Crush cookies and sprinkle with additional Cointreau. Gently twist jam jar and remove from the soufflé. Immediately fill the cavity with crushed cookies. Decorate around outer edge with remaining whipped cream and garnish with mint leaves. Refrigerate. Remove foil just before serving.
Hint: A few ice cubes placed in the jam jar will help soufflé set faster.

Fruit Compote

Makes 4 servings

1½ pounds prepared mixed fruit
   (strawberries, bananas,
   grapes, oranges)
½ cup red currants, stemmed
   Sugar
   Lemon juice

Slice or dice prepared fruit. Mix with red currants. Sprinkle to taste with sugar and lemon juice. Serve in individual bowls.

Floating Islands

Makes 4 servings

1½ teaspoons cream of tartar
5 egg whites
3 to 4 tablespoons fructose *or* sugar
1 cup Berry Sauce (recipe below)
Thin slices chilled mango, kiwi, *or* tiny fresh mint leaves, optional

In a 3 or 4-quart saucepan, bring 2 quarts water and cream of tartar to a boil. Reduce heat; keep water simmering. In a large mixing bowl, beat egg whites until soft peaks form. Slowly add fructose, beating until soft peaks form. With a spatula, mound ¼ of the whites onto a perforated skimmer and smooth gently into a dome-shaped "island." Gently place skimmer on the surface of the water until egg white is released and floats on the water. Rinse and dry the skimmer. Repeat for 3 more islands. Simmer 6 to 7 minutes; turn and simmer 6 to 7 minutes or until egg whites are set. Drain on a clean towel; cool. To serve, chill 4 dessert plates. Spread the Berry Sauce in the centers of the plates and place an island in the center of each. Garnish with fruit and mint, if desired.

Berry Sauce

Makes 1 cup sauce

¼ cup fructose *or* sugar
¼ cup water
½ pound fresh strawberries, raspberries, *or* blackberries *or* 1 10-ounce package thawed frozen berries
1 to 2 tablespoons lemon juice to taste *or* Kirsch *or* Cassis to taste, optional

In a bowl, dissolve fructose in water. Purée berries and sugar water in a blender or food processor. Strain sauce through a sieve, pressing the berries through with a spoon. Stir in lemon juice and Kirsch, if desired. Store covered in the refrigerator.

Helpful Hints

Turn small decorative bowls upside down and use as candle bases.

Melon Cocktail

Makes 4 servings

1 well-chilled medium honey-
   dew melon
¼ cup cream sherry
   Sugar, optional
   Lemon juice
   Maraschino cherries

Halve melon; remove seeds. Scoop out pulp with a melon baller; place in a bowl. Pour sherry over melon; sprinkle with sugar and lemon juice. Cover and refrigerate for about 1 hour. Transfer melon and juices to 4 stemmed glasses. Garnish with maraschino cherries.

Vacharin Fruit Tortes

Makes 4 servings

   Powdered sugar
5 egg whites
3 to 4 tablespoons powdered
   sugar
½ cup powdered cocoa or
   ground nuts
1 cup Creme Chantilly (recipe
   below)
2 cups raspberries, strawberries, or diced fruit of your
   choice
   Powdered sugar

Preheat oven to 350° F. Grease a baking sheet and dust with powdered sugar. Beat egg whites until they form soft peaks. Slowly add sugar until stiff peaks form. Fold in cocoa or nuts. Pipe or spoon mixture onto prepared baking sheet in 4 circles; with the back of a spoon make small wells in the centers. Bake in oven until set, about 10 minutes. Cool. Fill with Creme Chantilly and berries. Dust with powdered sugar. Chill and serve.

Creme Chantilly

Makes 4 servings

½ cup whipping cream
½ cup cream cheese
   Powdered sugar to taste
   Cognac to taste

Whip together cream and cream cheese. Flavor with sugar and cognac.

Melon Cocktail, this page

Strawberry Mousse

Makes 8 to 10 servings

4½ cups sliced strawberries
1⅓ cups sugar
1½ tablespoons cornstarch
2 tablespoons unflavored gelatin
⅓ cup Kirsch
2 cups whipping cream

Lightly oil a 2-quart mold; set aside. In a large saucepan, combine strawberries and 1 cup of the sugar. Bring to boiling, then cook over low heat, stirring constantly until sugar dissolves. Chill just until syrupy but not firm. Stir cornstarch and gelatin into Kirsch; let stand 5 minutes. In a small bowl, gradually add the remaining ⅓ cup sugar to the whipping cream, beating until stiff. Fold whipped cream into the strawberry mixture, then pour into the prepared mold. Refrigerate 8 hours. Unmold mousse onto a serving plate.

Chocolate Mousse Pie

Makes 6 to 8 servings

⅔ cup sugar
¼ cup cocoa
⅛ teaspoon salt
1 cup milk
1 envelope unflavored gelatin
¼ cup cold water
½ teaspoon vanilla
1 cup heavy cream, whipped
1 9-inch baked pastry or crumb pie shell

Combine sugar, cocoa and salt in a saucepan. Stir in milk and heat to boiling. Remove from heat. Dissolve gelatin in cold water and stir into hot mixture. Chill until mixture begins to thicken. Add vanilla. Fold in whipped cream and pour into pie shell. Chill until firm. Garnish with additional whipped cream if desired.